ENDORSE

"This book is a must-have for any parent who is struggling to understand, relate and parent their child to success in an ever-changing world that has made parenting extremely difficult, stressful and challenging. This book is an answer to that and is unique because it is written from the perspective of a child talking to their parents, which is pure gold for a parent who needs the answers and really cares. In reality, our children's evaluation of us matters the most, so why not get the answers first? Kristie and Kirstie do a masterful job in bridging the gap between parent and teen."

– Dr. Alduan Tartt
Child, Family, and Marriage Psychologist

"Teenager — the period of tension between puberty and maturity. The time of life when sex glands become functional, self-awareness becomes frightening and identity becomes a crisis. It is the time when experimentation is the rule and parents must keep it from becoming the pattern for life. In their new book, *Bridging the Gap: What Teens Wish Their Parents Knew*, Kirstie and Kristie Bronner take you on a tour of the teen mind, the seemingly illogical logic and irrational rationality. A must read for every parent wanting to level up their parenting toolbox!!"

– Dr. A. R. Bernard
Senior Pastor of Christian Cultural Center in Brooklyn, NY

"The Bible says that you know a tree by the fruit it bears, and I must say that Bishop Bronner and Dr. Nina Bronner are some amazingly rare trees in today's society. I have seen them flourish as amazing orators of the Gospel and I have personally been blessed by their ministry. When I first met Bishop Bronner, all of his children were transitioning. Some transitioning to college, some transitioning into motherhood, some transitioning into manhood as I remember it. I often wondered how their children would turn out with all the traveling, speaking engagements and the limelight placed on their world renowned ministry. I think we have all seen our share of preachers' kids not turn out as well as we thought they would. After seeing all five Bronner children flourish in this forever-changing world, I must say I am impressed. It challenged me to think "what's the secret?" In *Bridging the Gap*, their twin daughters do a phenomenal job of sharing their parents' best secrets to raising exemplary teenagers. This book is funny, inspiring, informative and hard to put down! By the time you finish reading this, I'm convinced you'll feel empowered and excited to embrace the challenges of raising exceptional teenagers."

–Willie Moore, Jr.
Nationally Syndicated Radio Host and Author

"I've been a teenager. My daughters and granddaughter have been teenagers. They can be confusing years for both parents and teens. The gap seems to enlarge almost overnight. Parents are not prepared for their teens and the teens don't understand what happened to their parents. Kirstie & Kristie (aka The Bronner Twins) have written *Bridging the Gap: What Teens Wish Their Parents Knew* that not only removes the mystique, but gives both parents and teens practical tools to grow together just like they had envisioned."

– Dr. Sam Chand
Leadership Consultant and author
of *New Thinking—New Future*

"The bond between parent and child can become strained during the teenage years. Kirstie and Kristie Bronner have given us a valuable resource that will help so many to not give up hope when the going gets tough. Thank you, ladies, for your unique insight and for literally *Bridging The Gap*!"

– Sheryl Brady
Pastor of The Potter's House
of North Dallas in Frisco, Texas

"The gap between parents and kids can be huge. I have raised two kids through this season and wish I had this kind of resource to help my wife and I during the tough teen years. In *Bridging the Gap: What Teens Wish Their Parents Knew,* Kirstie and Kristie take away the barriers that hinder teens and their parents from getting along. God made family to be a fun place. If you desire to improve your relationship long-term, this will help your family find a new level of unity. Children are, 'God's best gift,' (Psalms 127:3, Message Bible). This book will help both parents and teenagers understand each other in ways they were unable to before. Currently my kids tell me two things were important when they were teens, one was my presence and secondly, my patience. This is the time and the season to Bridge the Gap before it is too late."

– Dr. Ricky Temple
Senior Pastor of Overcoming
by Faith Ministries in Savannah, GA

Bridging the
GAP

Peace & Blessings,
Dr. Nina Brown

Developed from conversations and interviews with
over 500 parents and teens

What **Teens** *wish* their **Parents** knew

Bridging the
GAP

Kirstie and Kristie
The Bronner Twins, Authors of *Double Vals*

CARNEGIE
BOOKS

Bridging the Gap: What Teens Wish Their Parents Knew

Published by Carnegie Books

212 Riverside Parkway

Austell, GA 30168

carnegieenterprises7@gmail.com

Copyright © 2020 by Kirstie (Bronner) Foley and Kristie (Bronner) Brawley

Paperback Edition ISBN: 978-1-7332156-0-2

eBook ISBN: 978-1-7332156-1-9

Printed in the United States of America   1 2 1 7 1 9

ACKNOWLEDGEMENTS

In our father's book, *Power Principles*, he quotes Sir Isaac Newton saying, "If I have seen further, it is by standing upon the shoulders of giants." As our dad eloquently expresses his love and admiration for his parents as the giants in his life, he so perfectly describes our sentiments about him and our mother.

They are by far the wisest, godliest, most loving and generous people we know, and we couldn't be more proud to have them as the wind beneath our wings. We wouldn't be who we are without their being who they are. Their profound presence in our lives helps us to see more clearly, dream bigger, and love more deeply.

Bishop Dale C. Bronner and Dr. Nina Bronner, our parents, our giants, our hero and shero… You are some of God's greatest gifts to our lives and our destinies. Thank you for showing us God's heart for us by the way you live, for encouraging and supporting us endlessly, by believing in us before we knew to believe in ourselves, and for praying for us without ceasing. Sometimes you really do seem too good to be true, yet you remain honest, pure, and full of integrity.

We love you to life, forever.
Kirstie and Kristie

CONTENTS

Preface   ix

Chapter 1 The Epidemic of Our Society   1

Chapter 2 Is Your Home Healthy?   5
Dysfunction Defined   5
What Health Looks Like   17

Chapter 3 Powerful Language   23
Building Your Teen's Self-Image   23
The Prophetic Nature of Your Words   41
Affirmation   49
How NOT to Communicate   58

Chapter 4 Friend or Parent   69
The Beauty of Balance   69
How Strict is Too Strict?   79
The Keys to Openness   90
Active Listening & Respect   104

Chapter 5 T-I-M-E   115

Chapter 6 Teens in the Spotlight   127
What It's Like   127
Problems & Solutions   133

Chapter 7 Discipline that Works   149

Chapter 8 Purposeful Protection   163
   Sheltering Done Right   163
   What to Look out for   172

Chapter 9 Raising Great Decision-Makers   185
   The Foundation   185
   The Strategy   196

Chapter 10 The "C" Word   207

Chapter 11 Creating Your Family Culture   219

Chapter 12 Healing for Mom and Dad   235

Chapter 13 After You've Tried   255

About the Authors   261

PREFACE

Twin girls in their twenties with no teenagers of their own yet, writing a book on parenting? Some of you might be wondering: "What makes them think they know enough about parenting to write a book about it? What qualifies them to teach parents how to improve their parenting skills when these young girls have no teenagers of their own?" For all such questions, we have three answers...

1. Professional Experience

We volunteered in youth ministry for 7 years and have worked professionally with youth for an additional 6 years.

Beginning at age 15, we taught our peers (ages 14-18) in a weekly Sunday school class. After that, we were youth event co-ordinators at our church (of over 20,000 members). Now, we also serve as the youth and young adult pastors. Much counseling comes with this job. We counsel youth and, occasionally, advise their parents as well. Additionally, we serve as the founders and directors of the Elite 31 mentoring program for young ladies in high school and for young adult ladies.

Through the annual youth conferences that we have coordinated since 2011 (drawing 1,000+ students and growing each year), we have met countless youth from all over, including the "churched" and the "unchurched." Four years of interaction with peers in college also showed us the effects of parenting that persist into adult years.

As we continue to counsel teenagers and young adults, we hear a common root of their issues that is quite disturbing—family.

We have heard and continue to hear students' complaints and regrets. They often feel comfortable venting to us about their home lives and seeking advice for things that they are too afraid to confront their parents with. We have heard the horror stories, comforted through the tears, and encouraged youth towards change.

Also, in preparation for *Bridging the Gap*, we have conducted numerous interviews with teenagers, college students, and parents from various family backgrounds to include a variety of perspectives.

So note that, regardless of how outrageous some of the stories in this book seem, reality these days is stranger than fiction…

2. Our Offspring Advantage

Bridging the Gap is a unique opportunity for you to gain insight about what works in parenting from the teen's perspective. Often, when we hear about parenting, it is from the parents' perspective. But have you ever considered that even great parents don't always know what really clicked in their teen's mind? What actually worked?

Some successful parents might even be surprised to hear what some of their kids' defining moments were. Like, what do your kids remember as their turning points for better or worse in their upbringing? Even our own exceptional parents have been intrigued when we've shared with them the moments that had the greatest impact on us while growing up.

Parents are able to observe their teen's behavior, but they often have a very vague understanding of what exact tactics or even which statements actually got through to their child.

If you've ever been to a joint counseling session with a friend, family member, or spouse, you understand. Your perspective of your efforts and their interpretation of those same actions are typically quite different. Nevertheless, it is their perspective that shapes their own reality. The best way for parents to gather how their methods are interpreted is to hear it from the teen's mouth—hence, *Bridging the Gap*.

Think about it as if the parents are the chefs, and the teen is the entrée. Most cooks often just toss in ingredients as they go along, just like most parents kind of "go with the flow" of daily routine, whatever that looks like for them. Much like chefs, parents are often merely experimenting...

Many talented chefs don't follow recipes: they almost instinctively combine ingredients, and the food actually turns out well! On the other hand, when many others just "toss things in the pot," the meal might not be quite so tasty...

What we are saying is this: It is absolutely necessary to educate yourself in parenting. Even the most amazing chefs typically went to culinary arts school, learned from a cooking master, or at least researched on YouTube! And then you have those rare exceptions who got it all on their own through natural talent. But don't get your hopes up because that's a small minority! Haha!

Some people had exceptional examples as parents and hit the jackpot by mostly imitating them. Unfortunately, most parents cannot honestly say that they had an exemplary upbringing themselves.

Of course, there is no perfect recipe for raising good teenagers. Every child and every parent is different. Understand that perfection is just a myth that humans will never be able to attain! There are, however, universal truths that stand as keys to a healthy household, even in those notorious teenage years. These keys are what we will share with you.

3. Our Model Parents

Our exceptional parents are probably the most important qualifying factor for our writing a parenting book. In fact, you can look at it like we're writing the book in their stead, since we share many of their best parenting secrets!

They somehow managed to raise five exceptional teenagers who never rebelled in high school or went wild in college. All of us remained close to our parents and at least mostly heeded their counsel. Haha!

They raised twins who turned out as double valedictorians

of their college with matching 4.0 GPAs, and a son who received a full scholarship to Yale Divinity School on a graduate level! Even more remarkable is the fact that each of their married daughters (4) made it to the marriage altar as virgins, by choice and not by force of nature. We weren't just a crew of ugly ducklings. Haha!

All five kids, who are now adults, are healthy spiritually, emotionally, morally, physically, and have healthy relationships and even families of their own. Most of our parents' children are now teaching and leading others.

Our family has remained in close relationship with each other, and all of us carry deep admiration for our parents because of who they are and all they have invested.

Because of our analytical minds, we have not allowed much of their work with us to blindly pass us by. We have processed things along the way and have even made plans for how we will someday run our own households.

Our parents have laid a firm foundation for us, and we will stand on the shoulders of giants as we go forth to establish our own families. Appreciating this remarkable foundation, we want to share this, and more, with you.

The Bridge

Naturally, there are two sides to every story. We are not taking sides, but we're simply helping parents understand the mindset of their teenagers.

The differences in the way parents think versus the way their teens think have been made painfully obvious to us. For example, when parents have come to us crying about their teen's rebellion and soliciting our prayers because their kid has run away...

The teenager talks to us expressing just how misunderstood he/she feels and how the parent never listens to his/her pleas for attention, so frustration led to an escape plan. We realized that the parent wasn't crazy, but neither was the teen! There were missing links of communication and understanding.

We all know that kids don't always know what's best for them; but, we err when we ignore their voices. What are they thinking? What is the root of their behavioral issues? Are my parenting methods actually working? How are they processing what I'm teaching?

Are parents really listening to what's going on? Are they focused on the real issues, or are they just responding to symptoms? Our mission is to bridge the gap between parents and their teens.

Our Audience

Bridging the Gap is for parents and future parents. After all, an ounce of prevention is worth more than a pound of cure! Why wait until you need to use the information to educate yourself? It's far better to enter parenthood well-equipped and prepared.

Although this book is useful for kids of all ages, it specifically targets the "difficult" years—raising teenagers. Thus, the best time to start preparing is *before* they reach this age.

If you're already the parent of an adolescent, use this resource to sharpen your parenting skills because your kids are worth the effort!

Effective parenting requires intentionality, a vision for your family's success, and a plan of action to make that vision a reality. This vision should include things like character development, not just behavior modification; identity formation, not just impressive facades; and unconditional love and acceptance. *Bridging the Gap* will help you attain that vision.

Whether you're preparing for your parenting journey or seeking to repair your relationship with your teens, be encouraged. With wisdom and God's help, anything is possible! Look forward to a rewarding relationship with your teens that brings growth to them and joy to you. (Psalm 127:3, 5)

CHAPTER 1

THE EPIDEMIC OF OUR SOCIETY

A large rift has developed between parent and teen, filled with cobwebs of lies that destroy trust, communication, and therefore, the very foundation of healthy relationships.

We are in desperate need of healthy parent-teen relationships and effective parenting that develops responsible, integrous young people—the future of our society.

"God 1st, family 2nd, and business 3rd" was our grandfather's motto. That is how he taught his six sons to prioritize life. These days, many people give their families excuses for why they're too busy to be there, which translates to family as "You're too busy to care." The very thing that is most important often comes last on the "to-do" list.

The Symptoms

Many parents are frustrated with their teens because of their poor behavior, and their kids are disconnected from, resentful towards, and disrespectful to their parents. There are countless issues that occur, but here are just a few common ones…

As reflected on television and in teenage conversations, it has become socially acceptable for teenagers to tell "white lies" to their parents. Many parents expect this behavior and follow their child's claim with, "Are you telling me the truth…?" or "Now, if you're lying to me…"

Many daughters acquire a "secret" boyfriend and even sneak out to date him, putting themselves in dangerous and "unknown" territory (literally). Often, sexual immorality follows, along with damaged self-esteem for that young girl who just became another notch on a guy's belt.

Many teens smoke and even sell a little marijuana that their parents may or may not catch them with… Their priorities can change, academic performances decline, or they could even get in legal trouble as one thing leads to another.

Although many shrug this stuff off saying, "Kids will be kids," there are lasting consequences for poor decisions, some that are readily apparent and some internal. We can do better to protect and equip our teens for holistic success.

The Problem

In lieu of well-equipped parents, an immoral society is raising our children. Teens are learning their language, culture, wardrobe style and values from society. No society, no matter how wholesome (although most are not!), is equipped to raise your teens with the quality that you can when you apply wisdom.

This society cannot teach our children how to be successful, honest human beings. However, they do an effective job at making sure all citizens know a lot about subjects such as politics, sports, sex, drugs, alcohol, celebrities, and maybe even the importance of education. We see these topics permeated throughout television, music, radio, school, and more. But the voids are vast, and it's because we've bypassed the root of the problem.

Why is it that the schools, churches, and mentoring programs are trying desperately, and with less than ideal results, to teach the teens of our society what they should have learned at home? Many people have become alarmed at the state of our world right now and seek to solve the problems through non-profit organizations, benevolence on the streets, mission trips, and more.

While all these efforts are wonderful, and we do them too, each person must take care of his/her own family as first responsibility. If everyone did this right, we wouldn't even need many of the outreach programs that we labor so diligently to sustain.

We must realize that family is the very foundation of society, the first institution of learning, the birthplace for the creators of culture and leaders of our society.

If we can nurture in love, discipline based upon principle, transfer moral values, and teach responsibility, all in the home, much of the brokenness and chaos of our society would not exist. But how can teens truly receive the values of their parents if they barely even talk? If communication between parent and teen is breached, character development is hindered.

The home is the place that either criminals, perverts, lazy, and greedy people are developed, or doctors, pastors, and pure-hearted leaders are nurtured.

The Hope after Brokenness

If families are broken, it is logical that they produce broken children who grow up to be broken adults, who then become broken parents, and the cycle continues...

Hurt people hurt people, whether intentionally or unintentionally, so imagine the kind of broken society that broken families collectively create.

Broken families often produce teens who lack integrity and have low self-esteem, a sense of purposelessness, love voids, and much more.

Now, let's not be negative: The only purpose for exposing the epidemic of today's society is to reveal the need for change in order to motivate parents to do something different. There is no need to sulk over what's wrong when you have the power to change it—one parent at a time, one household at a time.

Hope and strategy are available, and all you need is humility and willingness to run with what you learn. Notice, we did not say "perfection."

Through purposeful parenting, we'll see healing, love, peace, and redemption touch our world like we've never seen before! Family should be our first priority after God, so there is no other work more important than this. In fact, it is our God-given privilege and duty. Parenting IS our job!

After all, the first command God gave to mankind was "Be fruitful and multiply." In other words, He told Adam and Eve to become *parents*.

The Preparation

It's amazingly unfortunate how often people in many societies plan more for weddings than marriages; more for college (academic) prep than for spiritual and emotional prep in that next phase of life; and more for the baby shower than for effective parenting.

But preparation is key. One of the most successful single mothers that we know became pregnant in college and then started doing research on parenting. She prepared so well that her family stands in sharp contradiction to the disheartening statistics concerning single-parent households. Her child's emotional, spiritual, relational, and financial health and maturity are the proof that her investment paid off.

Most parents either raise their kids how they were raised (whether dysfunctional or not) because that is all they know, or they do the exact opposite of what their parents did because they hated it. Some have great intentions and might even be strategizing, yet with outdated tactics that aren't being understood or received by today's youth. It's time for parents to be proactive in their preparation for effective parenting.

Let's bring health back to our society starting with YOUR home…

CHAPTER 2

IS YOUR HOME HEALTHY?

Dysfunction Defined

O ne time when I (Kirstie) was in elementary school, I got so angry with my parents that I grabbed a pile of panties, wrapped them in a t-shirt, put the sack over my shoulder, and flung the front door wide open as I dramatically "ran away."

I got to the stop sign up the street when I realized that maybe I had overreacted... Because I had no place to go! Haha!

Some issues are inevitable in life with kids, but that doesn't make your home dysfunctional.

It is possible to have a healthy, imperfect, loving, and properly functional family.

Let's use your body as an example: You could have a common cold and still be considered healthy overall; if your body is plagued with cancer to the point that you might not survive, your body is clearly deemed diseased. With this in mind, understand that every family has their issues. But what is your family primarily characterized by?

Let's take a moment to lift up the mirror to our families and do a home inspection! If you haven't started your own family yet, you'll see in this chapter what mistakes to avoid and then what foundational pillars to include for a healthy family. If you are already a parent, use this chapter for introspection and evaluation of your family's current condition.

Before we delve into building a foundation for or restoring the family, you must first recognize where you are. As the saying goes, **"A problem well-defined is a problem half-solved."** Are you aware of how healthy or dysfunctional your family is? How do your family members view the condition of your family? You might need to ask.

This chapter will help you identify the common signs of dysfunction so that you can evaluate the health of your family and assess how you need to grow. What does your family need to focus on in particular, and what will your goals be to cultivate health in the areas that are lacking?

What Does Dysfunction Look Like?

> *Well, for the past 30 years or so, I've had little to say to either of my parents, who are now both in their 80's. Of course, they wonder why they seldom hear from me—seriously, it's quite the mystery to them. It's not so much that I'm holding a grudge, though I can see how it might seem that way. It's more that I don't need or want their brand of toxicity in my life, because it just wears me down. Is that really so strange?* —Blogger

Notice that this quote is from an adult. This means that the dysfunction in the home during teenage years, when the child is actually living with his parents, can affect the health of family relationships indefinitely. Teens often make comments like the following:

"Ooo… I can't wait until I turn 18 and move out of this prison!!!" (in reference to your home!) Most teenagers have either said or thought something that parallels this concept.

How are parents to know if this feeling is merely a rebellious phase that kids go through, or if they've been making mistakes that provoked their teens to this point?

How do you know if your household displays the odd parent-teenager interaction that is considered normal, or if there is actually something wrong?

Webster defines dysfunction as "abnormal or unhealthy interpersonal behavior or interaction within a group." Is the interaction among your family members healthy?

> *My mother is illogical and irrational. She is beyond nosy and loves to eavesdrop on everyone else's private conversations... She... enjoys criticizing and... constantly jumps to conclusions that have absolutely no basis in reality. For her, the only "reality" that counts is the one she creates in her own mind. And don't even think about sharing with her anything you hold dear in your heart. She will... annihilate it for you. —Blogger*

The truth is that few parents actually intend to seem cruel, selfish, or unloving to their teens. What your kids interpret from your behavior is often different from what you'd hope. In fact, if you're taking the time to read this book, you obviously care about being a good parent. And you'd probably be shocked to discover how hurt your teen might be about something you didn't think was a big deal. Nevertheless, they could still be thinking the following about you:

> *My father... has little to say to anyone, until he gets on one of his bigoted tirades... You start to wonder if he's going to have a stroke, as his eyes bug out, his veins start bulging and his face turns purple. [He] is more of a seemingly dormant volcano that sometimes erupts unexpectedly... To disagree with either of my parents, who are clearly omniscient, by the way, is to be branded an idiot and, well, just plain wrong. —Blogger*

Unfortunately, it's all too common that teens feel like they're not allowed an opinion or like they've been robbed of a voice in their home. Simply put, they don't feel heard. This feeling tends to foster anger and distance between parent and teen.

Naturally, people are not perfect, so no family can be perfect. Even in healthy homes, teens will get upset with parents because of decisions that they don't understand, and parents will become angry with their kids because of foolish behavior.

Teens will say harsh things they don't mean, simply out of untamed emotionalism. Growing up, we can't even count the many times we said, "I hate you" to our siblings, complained to our mom about cleaning the kitchen, and got upset with our parents because they didn't like our friends.

However, we must take the time to distinguish *normal* struggles from dysfunctional ones. Dysfunctional families naturally produce dysfunctional individuals who leave home and sabotage relationships with others.

Every teenager does not have to be wild, rebellious, bubbling with hatred for their parents, and itching for the day when they can move out! And all parents don't have to yell until they turn red and destroy their children's self-confidence when they get frustrated.

The truth is that these common surface-level issues (e.g. constant rebellion and yelling in the home) are just a couple of symptoms of dysfunction. There are many signs of dysfunction in the family, and we need to understand that these things indicate the need for healing.

It goes without saying that problems like addiction and abuse (physical or verbal) are considered dysfunction in the home, but what else? Because awareness is the beginning of change, let's talk about it and see if you recognize your family in any of the following descriptions:

1. Unhealthy Communication

Constant fighting among family members makes the home environment feel like a war zone. To clarify, conflict is considered unhealthy when the choice of words is either nonexistent (a.k.a. "the silent treatment") or is damaging and discouraging. Both methods create further distance between family members.

When communication is poor, members of the family don't discuss many things that they should express, but they often find opportunities to say the hurtful things that should not be uttered. Unhealthy secrecy abounds in this environment.

The home does not feel peaceful, safe, calm, and welcoming: instead, it's unpredictable and unstable. It causes family members to feel uneasy, anxious, or angry. And typically, family members seek refuge elsewhere.

One Sunday morning, we talked with a teenager who expressed that she loves coming to church so much because it feels like home. It's the only place where she can feel safe and at peace. Her household is so chaotic that the word "home" is an inappropriate description for the place where she lives.

Although it's great to have a church home in addition to your family's home, when places like church, school, or a friend's house feel more like "home" than home, there's evident dysfunction.

2. Shame

It is completely normal for teens to feel embarrassed of the silly things their parents do sometimes or even embarrassed of the way they discipline. But, when your teens are vowing to never become like you; when they are ashamed to bring their friends around you; or when they're jealous of those who have happy families, you know there is dysfunction in the parent-teen relationship.

David: "Hey Blake, can we play video games at your house today? We always play at mine, and my parents are getting tired of us hogging the TV every day after school."

Blake: "Uhh, nah. In that case, I'll just head to Jim's house to play."

David: "What? So, you're just going to ditch me the one day I say we can't go to my house? What's really going on? I don't get it. Do your parents not like me or something? Is your house dirty? What is it, man?"

Blake: "I just don't want to, okay? What's with all the questions? Just forget it."

David: "Look Blake, I'm your friend. You can tell me the truth. Why don't you ever want me to come over your house?"

Blake: "[Sigh] Well, it's not you. I don't like for any of my friends to meet my parents. They fight with each other all the time and then end up dragging me into it if I'm around. Sometimes, they act like children, and I feel like I have to be the adult. It's embarrassing for my friends to come over because I never know if or when they'll have another episode. Just too much drama and too much risk... Not worth some stupid video games with friends..."

The parents' behavior in this example is clearly dysfunctional, and no child would be proud of that environment.

We've listened to numerous teens describe the irresponsible, hostile, foolish, and hurtful behavior of their parents, and we've heard many of them vow to never be like their own parents. Some of them even fear having children because of their experience.

It's evident that when teens are ashamed of their parents, and when their parents are exactly who they DON'T want to be in the future, there's a need for change.

3. Seeking "Family" Outside the Home

The family should be the first place that a child finds acceptance, love, a sense of identity, and support. Every human being has the need for these things. Therefore, if people don't feel like they receive these things at home, they will seek them elsewhere. This can lead to highly unhealthy relationships even outside of the family.

Sometimes the person lacking familial support and affirmation feels like he/she must be in a romantic relationship in order to be validated. Whether this relationship is healthy or toxic, people tend to cling to it because they feel like they *need* it.

Someone who fears being single is looking to others for

security, significance, and love. For example, a guy we knew grew up with a mother who humiliated him in front of others and created a hostile environment through a lot of yelling. He honestly didn't even want to call her "Mom."

As a 25-year-old man, he had only been single for 3 months at a time since childhood, and he married someone that he wasn't sure he was fully satisfied with because she gave him an ultimatum: he had to marry her or lose her. He wasn't sure if she was the best one, but he knew that she was someone.

The lack of identity, acceptance, and support within the family can also lead to a hyper-attachment to friends. In other words, the teen can become needy, chasing friendships even if the so-called "connection" is not mutual.

Have you ever been in a situation where you don't feel like you connect with someone, yet he/she pursues your friendship as if you're already best friends? Sometimes, not always, that person is seeking acceptance and validation that he/she never received at home.

The bad news is that depending on other people to fill emotional voids often leads to heartbreak and disappointment.

As freshmen in college, we had a friend, Ruth, who had a huge void because of her family dynamics, and she clung to a particular "best friend" right before she became close friends with us. Her friend's name was Ashley. In an effort to protect her heart, we encouraged Ruth to let go of Ashley's friendship.

Ashley would occasionally dodge Ruth's phone calls for disrespectful reasons; she would lie to her; and she would stand Ruth up when they were scheduled to meet. Over and over, Ashley would take advantage of Ruth's kindness, and every time Ashley came crawling back with apologies, Ruth would receive her.

One day, Ashley told Ruth that she would meet her at their school's cafeteria. Needless to say, she never showed up. Ruth waited and waited until she had finished all of her food and decided to head back to her dormitory.

On the campus shuttle, as she was headed back to her room,

feeling lonely and abandoned, she spotted Ashley on the shuttle with a group of her new friends. Shocked and hurt, she approached Ashley. To Ruth's bewilderment, Ashley looked her in the eyes and continued laughing with her friends, as if she didn't know her.

Later, Ruth cried to the two of us about the situation until she couldn't cry anymore. We told her to give the relationship some space and evaluate her dependence upon Ashley.

Against our advice, she continued to call Ashley and leave her voicemails until Ashley apologized. With a simple apology, Ruth attempted to mend their friendship and pretend like the offense never happened.

After a few more sad instances like this one and after many more tears, Ruth finally severed the relationship and moved on. For many years past this point, she still used her friendships to fill her family void and stay out of the house as much as possible.

For some, it's friends, boyfriends, or girlfriends in an attempt to fill the family void, and others reach further to seek gangs, clicks, or even casual sex with various people at the expense of their morality, safety, or health.

The person who is seeking other people or things to fill the place of his/her family often tries to stay away from home as much as possible, sometimes to engage in positive activities and other times unspeakable things… whatever gets the job done.

But home should be a place of love, support, peace, and loyal relationships. If not, there is work to be done.

4. Strained Parent-to-Parent Relationship

When a teen's parents have a poor relationship with each other, it can make the child feel unsafe, hurt, and even rejected. He/she starts to feel like nothing is really secure.

It's undoubtedly ideal for parents to be married to each other. And marriage should be enthusiastically celebrated! But when married parents are constantly fighting, lacking affection, and maybe even sleeping in different beds for years, it strips kids of their example of what normal, loving parents look like—what *family* looks like.

To all married parents who are struggling to get along, we strongly encourage you to fight for your marriage. Fight for each other like you would for your kids that you love so much. That's what family does.

Pressures of this life tend to cause people to focus on negativity, especially in those closest to them. The truth is, all humans will make mistakes and cause disappointment; but through prayer and counseling, you can better understand each other and restore your bond. **You can *choose* to love each other: It's called commitment.**

If your so-called "unconditional" love for each other has hidden conditions, how can your teen trust your unconditional love for him/her? How can your kids feel secure in the family's love if you, the parents, stop loving each other?

Divorce

So, what if you're already divorced? If parents are divorced or never married, the kids still need to see a healthy relationship between mother and father. They shouldn't hear mom cursing out dad and talking about everything he lacks. Neither should they be forced to pick sides.

Divorce is far too common and life-altering. Nevertheless, strong, healthy families can still be maintained in the midst. It is rare because it requires powerful maturity, but it is possible.

One particular family experienced divorce when the kids were young, and then both parents married others. It took the kids a while to get adjusted to the new mother and father figures, but the biological parents always showed kindness and respect to each other.

The kids spent an abundance of time with both biological parents and step-parents, and their environment was very loving and stable. The biological parents always demonstrated great maturity in their relationship and could comfortably be in the same room for peaceful family functions.

For these situations to work, forgiveness must take place, and parents must show respect for each other. The teens in the above example love both parents (including step-parents) dear-ly, and they greatly value family time.

The bottom line is that kids need stability in the home. Alt-hough it is most ideal for parents to be married, single and di-vorced parents can still work together for the good of the family.

Single-Parent Homes

A particular example of a healthy single-parent household began with a girl who became pregnant during her senior year of college. She was determined that her daughter would not have a poor life or dysfunctional family just because of her mis-take.

Although she did not continue in romantic relationship with her child's father, she intentionally did not argue with him in her daughter's presence, and she refrained from speaking negatively about him to her daughter. In fact, she spoke of only the positive things about him and actually encouraged her daughter to love him.

She did not make her emotional weight become her daugh-ter's burden, but she chose to put her daughter's well-being be-fore her own feelings. She actually planned annual "family" va-cations with her "ex" and her daughter, so that her daughter could have that experience.

This growing girl never felt abandoned by her dad because her mother invited him into her life. Despite the fact that her daughter's father was her ex-boyfriend, she didn't selfishly keep her daughter from his family either. She figured, the more family support her daughter had, the better.

Today, her daughter is a successful, wise, committed Christian in a healthy romantic relationship. She is responsible, and she is confident in her identity in Jesus and within her family.

This did not happen by accident. To foster such amazing re-sults, you must be intentional. And because single-parent households are often highly dysfunctional, single parents must be mindful to avoid the common mistakes and make wise decisions.

The single parent who is actively dating should avoid frequent visitors to the home. Often, rape and molestation of the children occur in these scenarios. And if there must be company, the parent should always be present.

> *Doing what others aren't willing to do is the bridge to exceptionality.*

Also, kids should not have "father" and "mother" figures walking in and out of their lives. This instability is harmful to the hearts and minds of children. Therefore, you should establish boundaries for your dating experience.

The story of the successful single mother mentioned above also includes intentionality in this area. This mother discussed with her daughter's father a rule for both of them—they will not introduce their daughter to the parents' girlfriends and boyfriends.

The daughter was not to meet a new person until "you're getting ready to walk down the aisle" (said the mother). This means that home is a safe place with familiar faces and people who actually stick around. They both adhered to this rule during their daughter's upbringing.

When the relationship is approaching marriage, the parent should initiate conversation with the teen about his/her feelings concerning the significant other. The teen needs to know that he/she is valued in the conversation. This kind of inclusion translates as "You are important to me."

Realize that it is possible for the parent-teen relationship and parent-parent relationship to be healthy, even in this context. It requires prayer and wisdom. **Doing what others aren't willing to do is the bridge to exceptionality.**

When asked what advice she would give to other single parents, this successful single mother said to eliminate excuses. She stated, "[This] is not an excuse for dysfunction. It just means you have to work differently."

When she became pregnant out of wedlock, she began

reading books about parenting, doing biblical studies about it, and seeking to learn how to be the best parent she could be. She chose to be intentional and decide her family's mission.

She also shared that she prayed and asked God for strategy. Specifically, she prayed for a "village": she prayed that God would send the right support system of men and women to help teach her daughter.

God answered, and she had a list of people that her daughter could call if she didn't want to talk to just "Mom." Her daughter was then able to spend time with other positive married couples and observe what a healthy marriage looks like.

Again, being a single parent does not have to mean you raise a dysfunctional family. You have a choice. But, it's vital that you understand what constitutes a healthy family. Then, you have the tools to start building!

IS YOUR HOME HEALTHY?

What Health Looks Like

What Is a Healthy Family?

Let's start by clarifying that, when we say "healthy" family, that is not code for "perfect" family. The latter does not exist.

As stated above, even healthy families still have issues, but what is your family primarily characterized by? This is what determines if your family is considered healthy or dysfunctional.

Now that we've established that healthy families are not perfect, we must also be clear about the ingredients for a healthy family. Yes, there are many variables according to the nature of your family, but there are also fundamental elements that must be present. We will briefly overview some of those characteristics.

Received Love

Sarah: "My mom doesn't love me."

Kirstie: "What do you mean, your mom doesn't love you? I'm sure she does."

Sarah: "She never hugs me, kisses me, or spends a lot of time with me like my friends' moms. She only tells me that she loves me every now and then. And when she does, it feels awkward."

[Note that this is a conversation that actually occurred. Like the others in this book, the name of the teen has been changed for anonymity.]

In this scenario, the teen did not understand her mother's expression of love. Make sure that, regardless of the ways you communicate your love, it is clearly recognizable.

Every healthy family gives and receives love in ways that the family members understand. Of course you love your children, but are they confident of that? Some kids say they rarely hear the words "I love you" and don't feel the love. Realistically, a family cannot possibly be healthy if the family members do not feel loved by each other.

Pretty much all parents love their children, but we have

heard far too many teenagers admit that they don't think their parents actually love them. This means that love in the parent's heart is not enough to make a healthy home. It must be communicated and demonstrated in a way that the kids understand so that they actually feel loved and accepted in the family.

Some people are highly physically affectionate, some are mildly affectionate, and some hardly; but, whether you hug and kiss all day and constantly say, "I love you" or not is dependent upon your family culture and the love languages of your family members.

We've heard numerous teens express that their father buys them clothes, jewelry, game systems, and more trying to "make up" for the time that he does not spend with them. The reality is that the father is expressing his love through gifts while his children are yearning for his demonstration of love through quality time.

Kids should never have to question whether or not their parents love them and are proud of them. Remember that people's personalities are different, and therefore, they receive love in different ways. You might even need to ask your kids what communicates love to them (i.e. acts of service, words of affirmation, physical affection, gifts, quality time). Whatever the conclusion is, love must be expressed to your teens the way they understand it, just like you want your spouse to love you the way you recognize love.

If you don't feel comfortable vocalizing your affection, consider writing it. Occasionally, send thoughtful text messages or write heartfelt letters or emails. If they need acts of service, plan to do something unusually kind for them that they didn't ask for. If they desire more quality time, try scheduling parent-teen dates doing whatever activity they want. Even consider taking each child out individually to make him/her feel special.

Speak your teens' love language to ensure that they are always confident of your love and their priority in your life. It won't always be convenient or easy, but it is of the utmost importance. **Remember that love constitutes the bricks with which a healthy home is built.**

Discipline

Also essential to a healthy family is discipline, which we can think of as correction for the purpose of maturation and development. Parents must play the role of parents and provide necessary guidance to their children.

Teens need correction and wise counsel. They also need the protection that a wise parent's parameters provide.

Too often, we've heard teens say something like this: "I can do whatever I want. My parents don't care." Believe it or not, the lack of discipline also communicates a lack of love. Although kids don't like discipline, they need it, and they'll miss your concern and attention if they don't have it.

When teens don't have established parameters, they feel unsafe, and left to find their own way. Parents must demonstrate concern for who their children will become and discipline them so that the prison system doesn't have to.

See the "Discipline that Works" chapter for more details about discipline.

Transference of Values

In addition to the "what-not-to-do" of discipline, teens need the "what-to-do," as in the transference of values, priorities, and morals. Much of this is learned through the example of the parents, intentionally or unintentionally.

Why? Because the home is the first institution of learning. Parents have more influence on their kids than anyone else. Understand this influence, and use it wisely to develop people of integrity.

We discuss this more extensively in the "Creating Your Family Culture" chapter.

Remember that love constitutes the bricks with which a healthy home is built.

Positive Self-Image

Most kids first identify themselves as who their parents tell them that they are. Healthy families are environments in which growing children should develop a positive self-image. Is a positive sense of identity encouraged and developed in your home?

Our parents did an amazing job of encouraging a positive self-image in us. Before we knew who we were, our parents made us believe that we could do anything and be anybody we so desired.

Through frequent verbal affirmation and corresponding behavior, they had already made us confident that we were loved by them and by God. Because of them, we just KNEW we were special, gifted, mature, and even good-looking people! They made us believe that we were far beyond average and that we were destined for greatness.

Always encourage a positive sense of identity in your teens. Kids with positive self-images make healthier, happier homes and more productive and peaceful societies!

For details about how to strategically shape your kids' identities, see the "Powerful Language" chapter.

Parental Admiration

Also, in a healthy home, the teens should admire the leadership and character of their parents. Girls should be able to learn from their mothers how to be great women, wives, and moms; and, boys should be able to learn from their fathers how to be great men, husbands, and dads.

Many kids reach a point where they think: "I need a mentor, someone to teach me how to be a man/woman!" In fact, a particular young adult has told us several times things like, "Dang, I feel behind... Why am I just now learning this stuff about being a woman [from you]? Why didn't my mom ever teach me this stuff?"

Well, doesn't every child have a mom (example of a woman) and a dad (example of a man)? Yes... and no. Not all kids feel like they have a great example to follow and someone they can openly discuss the intimate matters of their lives with to gain counsel, direction, and inspiration for future success.

Despite the differences in our personalities, our mother has always been the woman we most aspire to be like. We have seen her in the good times and the bad. And, the consistency of her character, her humility when she's wrong, and her grace and love in hurtful situations still astound us. She has shown us how to be better wives than we could've ever been without her example, and, one day, we aspire to be at least close to the caliber of mother that she is.

Our brother also admires our father, loves to spend time with him, and is becoming more like him day by day. How amazing it is to have your "hero" and "shero" living under your same roof!

All parents should seek to carry themselves in such a way that their teens are filled with natural admiration. One of the best indicators to parents that they are doing at least a decent job is if they have gained the respect, trust, and admiration of their children to the degree that their own teens can look no further than home for their role model.

We are not saying that youth seeking mentors outside the home is an automatic red flag. People get mentors for different reasons, even certain professions/crafts/skills, meaning seeking another mentor is not a problem. In fact, it is highly beneficial for them to gain additional insight beyond the scope of only their parents' experience. The main point is that your teen should not need to look for a mentor to simply teach him/her the things that parents are designed to give to their children.

Evaluating and Moving Forward

Contrary to most pastors' kids, whose stereotypical image is either wild or socially awkward, we were neither. We were not suffocating and struggling to break free, nor were we living in a bubble of isolation. We loved our home environment.

It wasn't perfect, but we had healthy communication, a whole lot of love, faithful support, effective discipline, and necessary freedom to practice our decision-making skills.

Sure, when you are living with people, you are guaranteed to see their faults and become annoyed and frustrated with them occasionally. And sometimes, out of teens' immaturity, they cannot understand decisions made on their behalf that are in their best interests. This will lead to tension and frustration at times. Nevertheless, teens can still have a healthy relationship with their parents.

Both of us and our siblings have seen our parents' flaws, of course, and even disagreed with some of their decisions. But, we have still learned all of our greatest lessons from them, received our greatest counsel from them, and gained unfailing respect for them.

Nevertheless, we must all understand that perfection is not the goal, nor is it attainable. If it were the goal, we'd spend our entire lives itching for change that will never come!

Even if a teen were raised in seemingly perfect conditions, he/she could still rebel due to temptation, natural weakness, and free will. Teens won't be perfect. For example, despite our amazing parents, we and our siblings made some really dumb choices sometimes!

Some things you just can't control. But let's focus on what you can do. Learn all you can, grow, invest in your teens, and work hard at this job called parenting. All the while, trust God with what you cannot control. After all, He is the only perfect One.

Identify the areas that need improvement in your home; understand what a healthy family looks like; and work toward resolution. Try sitting down for a real conversation with your family members, asking important questions, and letting everyone express themselves.

Then, when you have become more aware of your family's condition, choose one thing for your family to improve. Take it one step at a time, and one day at a time. Change won't come overnight, but through process. And keep in mind that professional counseling is always an option if the situation is too much for you to handle.

Remember, awareness is the beginning of change, so hopefully your progress has already begun! Stay encouraged and persistently pursue health for your family.

CHAPTER 3

POWERFUL LANGUAGE

Building Your Teen's Self-Image

Exhibit A: "She called me stupid one time, and I happened to have a test to study for... I remember feeling like I wasn't going to be able to do well on that test."

[Although this student's mother apologized, this young girl distinctly remembered this situation into her adulthood.]

Exhibit B: "B*tch and stupid are the two main words I was called that I vow I will never call my children. She called me a hoe one time, not because I was behaving like one, but because she was mad. It wasn't often, but it hurt."

Exhibit C: "One time my mom and I got into an argument, and she said, 'You aren't much to look at.'"

Exhibit D: One night after our Thursday evening youth service, a young lady captured our attention with a long, tight hug accompanied by a downtrodden face. Without being prodded, she offered the story of her mother calling her an "ungrateful little b*tch" in the store.

"I know she was frustrated, but that really shocked me and hurt me," she said.

Exhibit E: "You're nasty!" This mother called her daughter nasty because she wasn't satisfied with the cleaning around the house that her daughter had done. She added to that the nickname, "Old MacNasty," which she repeated several times, to her daughter's dismay.

This exclamation of a mother toward her daughter caused more damage than one might realize. Her daughter's hurt over this statement still hadn't dissipated after years had passed.

"Sticks and stones may break my bones, but words will never hurt me." L-I-E!!! Bones heal faster than self-esteem does and probably faster than most of the broken relationships in the world.

What you say replays over and over again in your teen's mind like a looped music track.

Have you ever considered just how powerful and influential your words are in the lives of your teens? Your position as the one who is supposed to love and protect them causes your words to affect them even more than the words of many others, including their peers.

Now, we're not saying that teens are always innocent victims in this story, and parents are the villains. Sure, teens will misbehave and frustrate their parents. But, poor behavior does not justify destructive words from the "mature party" (a.k.a the parent). The goal is to develop your teens' character, not to taint their self-image.

One of the teenage guys in our youth ministry came to us explaining why he hadn't been around for the past couple of months. He was normally volunteering every week at the youth service. He was a very quiet guy, but he did more talking this night than we had ever heard him do.

He explained that he and his mom had been in conflict. They had both said damaging things to each other. His mom told him that he had been acting like trash. This statement pierced his heart, and in turn, he cursed at her. He felt extreme remorse for his behavior because he loved and respected his mother immensely.

He was a tall, husky athlete who normally showed no emotion; but, after this, his heart was torn. He said that, usually people's words don't affect him; but, because it was his mom who said it, it certainly did.

The great weight of parents' words means great responsibility, but also it means great privilege. You have the opportunity to choose how you will use this very precious tool called your tongue.

Since communication is the basis of all relationships, and communication shapes mentality and influences behavior, this chapter is one of the most important ones to digest.

In section 1 of this chapter, "Building Your Teen's Self-Image," you will discover how to properly shape identity with your words; how to utilize holistic affirmation in order to avoid breeding insecurity in your children; how to help your teens guard a good reputation; and, how to "trick" your kids into believing that (and therefore behaving as) they're exceptional people.

In section 2, "The Prophetic Nature of Your Words," you will learn how to help them discover their destiny using your words; how to strategically name your newborns; and how to utilize confessions to build their confidence.

In section 3, "Affirmation," you will understand the impact of what you *don't* say; the small things that really matter; the different methods of communication for different parent personalities; and the power of affirmation.

Lastly, in section 4, "How NOT to Communicate," we reveal detrimental words, detrimental questions, and detrimental methods of getting your point across.

The Power of Labels

"Wow! You have twins! Double trouble!" said many people to our parents from our double stroller days onward. Our parents immediately corrected them by lovingly responding, "No, double blessing!"

Whether it was a joke or not, our parents would not allow

people to negatively label us, even before we could understand what their words meant. They declared over us what they wanted our character to manifest, not simply the popular rhyming phrase to call twins.

Unfortunately, many parents not only allow others to negatively label their children, but they also degrade their kids' self-image with their own tongues!

"You are always the one getting in trouble!"

"I knew it had to be you who did it because it's always you!"

"You need to stop being so bad!"

Negatively labeling teens is a classic mistake that many parents make. It's extremely common to find households that have a "bad child," "trouble child," or even a "stupid child" that the parents and/or siblings have labeled.

As kids, we knew a girl who was the "bad child" of her family, and we observed the way that the label affected her attitude and actions. Yes, she did get into trouble often, but we were there to witness the times when she was falsely accused.

She wasn't even around when the incident happened, yet she was forced away from her sleepover with us to spend the night in her mother's bed. This is because her family always assumed that every bad thing that happened must've had her fingerprints on it!

Although she was upset when her mother ignored her as she denied the accusations, she was not surprised. She had grown accustomed to it. Because she felt like she would be blamed for trouble whether she was guilty or not, she eventually gave up trying to do the right thing. In her mind, what was the point? "If I'll get blamed regardless, I might as well stop wasting my energy trying." She eventually grew to embody her label as the "bad child" to a greater and greater extent.

Whenever you are tempted to assign a negative label to one of your children, remember the following principle: **Labels assigned by key people, like parents, tend to develop the character of the teen into the nature of the label.**

A funny story that proved the verity of this principle, in our own family, began at the dinner table one day. We were all in conversation about something when our dad said with a feigned tough attitude, "Kirstie and Kristie don't play!" He was saying this in a playful way, meaning that we didn't tolerate certain kinds of behavior from people. 😊

In order to avoid negative labels, always separate the person from the action.

This concept could later be applied to our high standards for ourselves and to those working with us on projects of any kind. We were skillful with words and serious about all of our endeavors, so it would be wise for someone not to get out of line. Haha! Since this quality wasn't fully demonstrated until later, he probably saw very small signs of this and just thought it was funny.

We had never thought of ourselves as being feisty, since most people had only described us as being sweet. And, although we knew that our dad didn't mean any harm by his playful statement (said with a chuckle and in a funny voice), his statement began to resound repeatedly in our minds.

Next thing we knew, if someone did or said something that they shouldn't have, "Kirstie and Kristie don't play" resurfaced in our minds, and we began to respond more aggressively than before!

At some point, we realized that we had become much more feisty since that moment, and we began our attempt to pull back a bit.

Our dad would have been shocked to discover that his simple joke affected our mentality the way it did. But this is a clear example of the weight that parents' words carry.

It's a good thing he and our mom positively affirmed our identity so often that we couldn't possibly forget!

It is true that whether good or bad, what parents say will

consciously or subconsciously affect the minds and subsequent behavior of their teens. Therefore, you should choose your words wisely…

In order to avoid negative labels, always separate the person from the action. One of your mottos concerning your children should be, "You aren't what you do." An individual's life should not be valued based upon his/her performance, whether good or bad.

When your teens behave poorly, you should be the one to remind them who they are: "This misconduct is not you. You are smart, talented, kind, and mature. What's really going on?"

This means, do not hold your teens' mistakes in front of their eyes like it's their identity. If you catch a child in a lie two or three times, beware of calling him/her a liar. If your teen thinks you believe he is a liar, he will probably give you just that. But, when he still sees his goodness through your eyes, he has higher standards to strive for. Otherwise, he'll likely settle for the negativity of his current choices.

There were many things we did not do because we so valued our parents' opinion of us. We wanted them to be proud of us and hated to ever disappoint them. We would not have cared about disappointing them if we didn't think they thought highly of us. With this in mind, when your teens make mistakes, never make them feel like you're *not* surprised.

This does not mean you should overreact to the mistake and make a big scene about it. Of course, you acknowledge their humanity—humans make mistakes. Nevertheless, you respond in a way that corrects and uplifts instead of attacks and discourages.

Because you expect more of them, you should never treat them like a certain kind of mistake is typical of them. As soon as they think that they're stigmatized that way, you're guaranteed to see more of that behavior.

You must make sure that your teens believe you think highly of them, even if you are struggling to view them in a positive light at the time. Your choosing to see the best in them is your responsibility, and they do not have to be involved in that process. Use your positive self-talk to redirect your thoughts and even pray that God will help you to see your teens how He sees them. They should always feel that, in your eyes, they are loved, accepted, and destined for greatness.

Well-Rounded Compliments

What if the beautiful compliments that you're showering upon your children can be both thoughtful and harmful at the same time?

Have you ever considered that one-sided compliments can have a limited benefit in your teens' minds? This was actually brought to our attention during an interview with a pastor's son who said that he suffered with severe low self-esteem as a child.

To our surprise, he admitted that his parents affirmed him a lot, but they were very limited in their affirmations to him. Most of their compliments included statements like the following: "You're a mighty man of valor." "You're a man of God." "You're a child of the Most High." He knew that God loved him already, but he wasn't confident about his personal traits that people would find valuable.

His parents spent little time letting him know that he was intelligent, gifted, handsome, creative, or any other such compliments. This pastor's son brought to light an interesting point: Parents must cater to the entirety of the child's being, not just his spirit or his physical appearance, for example.

Another one-sided affirmation that's all too common is performance-based praise. **Simply put, a job well done or poorly done is not WHO they are.** For instance, you never want to make your kids feel like they're more loved because they make good grades or less loved because they struggle academically. This perspective derives from an identity based upon performance.

It's great to encourage all positive behavior and achievements because you will get more of what you encourage. But, avoid emphasizing one positive thing about them so much that they feel like, if they don't measure up in that area at some point, they will lose your affection.

Think about it: Let's say your teen's name is Sam, and he does exceptionally well in school. Imagine that the only affirmations he hears from you are, "Ooo, Sam, you're our little smarty pants! You're so intelligent. What a little genius we have!" Doesn't it seem natural that he would feel extremely insecure to admit to you if he made a C+ in a class that he genuinely needs tutoring for?

Although this particular subject is an area of weakness for him, he might be too nervous to admit to you that he needs help. If his academic achievements have become his identity, he'd understandably be afraid to jeopardize his reputation and corresponding self-worth.

Again, don't be mistaken: It is a good thing to repeatedly praise good behavior and positive accomplishments. All we're emphasizing here is that there shouldn't be one particular aspect of the person that is exaggerated to represent how you feel about him overall.

Teens should be affirmed based upon constant factors, not just the things that can change at any moment. They should feel that they're accepted and loved for who they are, not because of anything they have or have not done.

Always remember to affirm the character of your teen, not just his behavior. For example: "Sam, you are such an amazing person! Your heart is golden, and you are so responsible and mature! I really appreciate your being such a joy."

This sounds simple to do, but based upon a parent's personal view of where self-worth lies, his/her compliments can naturally have a strong bias. Stereotypically speaking, imagine the affirmations of a model to her daughter versus those of a computer technician: "Sweetie, you are the most beautiful girl I've ever laid eyes on!" versus "You're so smart, Son. You can do anything you put your mind to."

Also, because of the influence of American society and

possibly even the world, females' value is typically placed in their appearance and males' in their possessions and abilities. These are still not the only areas in which each gender needs affirmation.

Our parents definitely did not focus on affirming us in just one aspect. Concerning our physical appearance, our father called us beautiful, gorgeous, and more. Our mother said so much in this department that, if we truly believed every word, we would all be conceited. Haha!

Although you might be appalled at some of her comments, these made us less susceptible to manipulation through flattery of men. We didn't have those googly eyes with everyone who called us beautiful like, "Oh really? You think so... Wow! [I'll do anything you want if you'll just tell me again!]" (drool...). And, we were not desperate for affirmation from males.

Now, this doesn't mean we never had insecurities or desired male attention. But, still, this helped. The following is just a short sample of the comments our mother repeatedly made while we were growing up:

- "Any man would be crazy to not want to be with you."
- "Any man would be glad to have you."
- "You're too beautiful to look at."
- "You're every man's dream."
- "It is no surprise that he wants to marry you— anyone would."
- "When guys tell you that you're fine/good-looking, you should think to yourself, 'I know!'"

Some of you might be judging right now, thinking, "Well, I certainly don't want to make my teens arrogant!" The truth is that, from television, classmates, and even close friends some-times, people are degraded, negatively compared, and discour-aged. What they don't get at home, they will seek elsewhere in a much more dangerous, manipulative environment.

We knew humility because our parents modeled it, and because they raised us with such strong values that we had what was most important at the forefront of our minds. Our household was not a shallow one: that's for sure.

Imagine if our parents only affirmed us in our outward appearance: To this day, our lives could be built on vanity because of a lack of confidence in our intelligence, talents, and spirit.

Because they wanted us to have the confidence to become leaders and not followers, they encouraged us accordingly. They regularly affirmed our ability to make good decisions and stand for what's right.

Below are examples of common affirmations that our parents spoke to us and to our siblings:

- You're very mature for your age.
- You're very wise.
- Great job!
- I'm proud of you.
- You can be anything you want to be.
- I respect who you are.
- You're a gift to this world.
- The world will be a better place because you lived.
- You can do anything.
- Your options are limitless.
- I couldn't have asked God for better children.
- You're such a gift to us.
- Working hard and praying, you can achieve anything.
- You're special and rare.
- I'm proud to be your dad/mom.
- I wouldn't trade you for any other kid.
- I love you.

Our parents also greatly affirmed our intelligence. Ever since we were young kids, we aspired to attend Spelman College because that was the prestigious school that our mother graduated from. In our eyes, it was the best school in the world!

Because of who she was to us, in addition to the great things we heard by word of mouth, we thought that Spelman was only for the smartest women. It seemed awesome and yet difficult to attain.

Although she never forced her alma mater on us, we dreamed of attending this school because we admired her so much; thus, we assumed that, of all the schools she had to choose from, if she chose this one, it must be the absolute best!

Eventually, we began doubting ourselves, wondering if we were smart enough to attend such a highly selective, private institution. As soon as she heard our insecurities, she stopped us: "You two are intelligent! You can go to any school you want to." She affirmed us in this manner all the way from our doubtful elementary school conversation to our acceptance to Spelman College during senior year of high school.

Another area that parents must affirm is what every human being yearns to know— "Why am I here, and what do I have to offer to the world?" Affirm the gifts and talents that you see in your teens. Tell them that they are talented and able to do anything they put their minds to. Tell them that their talents are special.

Point out to them the great qualities that they offer to those around them. For example, "Your joy is so inspiring. Every time you enter the room, you light it up!"

Identify the gifts that might lead to their future career and the gifts they offer to others in relationships. For example, some people are naturally and uniquely gifted as encouragers.

Our father noticed that our oldest sister often sent people encouraging text messages when she was a teenager. He pointed that out and repeated it throughout the years: "Dalina is so encouraging! She is a natural at making people feel good about themselves."

As a result, she has grown in that quality, and everyone

knows her to be an encouraging friend who always brings a smile and inspiring words! **Help your teens understand what they uniquely offer to the world, regardless of how seemingly small the gift might be.**

Make sure they understand that every single person has a purpose. God created all of us to glorify Him, and we do that in various ways, using our God-given gifts, personalities, and resources.

When you strategically affirm your kids in every area of their being, you will lay a healthy foundation for their identity in adulthood. And, when you affirm your love for your teens based simply on who they are, they can feel confident and secure. They feel supported enough to soar high, despite the odds against them, and accepted enough to seek your comfort and counsel when they do fall. Strategically use your words to uplift your teens' identity.

Respect Their Reputation

Next to affirming your teens' identity is nurturing their reputation. It is for good reason that the Bible says, "A good name is rather to be chosen than great riches" (Proverbs 22:1). We should care about our reputations, and it is very beneficial for your teens to care about theirs too.

The more your teens care about their reputation, the harder they will work to protect it. **As your teens work to protect their reputations, they will automatically be improving their behavior.** Because of this truth, *you* need to protect their reputation as much as you can. We've seen numerous parents make the classic mistake of exposing all of their kids' flaws to friends and strangers.

* * *

Help your teens understand what they uniquely offer to the world, regardless of how seemingly small the gift might be.

* * *

We've felt such compassion for teens as their parents say things like...

"I need to have you ladies talk to my daughter: she doesn't listen to me anymore these days, and she won't talk to me at all. Her attitude has been giving me a headache. She has been acting out in school, lying, and being rebellious. I guess it's just a phase she's going through, but I need some help. I need you girls to rub off on her."

The conduct of a teen who respects himself/herself is drastically different from one who does not.

How do you think her daughter felt, standing there being talked *about*, not to, right in her face? When statements like these are made, the teens tend to look away in shame and embarrassment, or look down to the floor trying to emotionally and mentally escape the situation. It's usually obvious that the teens are used to that kind of thing, and they're just doing what they normally do—mentally exiting the conversation.

Instances like these automatically degrade the child's reputation. Try not to speak for them as if they don't have a voice, especially when your words are negative. If you are actually seeking counsel for your teens, go to the counselor in private and talk to him/her outside of your teens' presence.

Our parents abided by the motto, "Praise in public and correct in private." Using this model, they protected our reputation. Your teens' reputation is relevant to their behavior because it typically influences their self-respect. **The conduct of a teen who respects himself/herself is drastically different from one who does not.**

Often, adults don't value respecting young people. Although we are all taught to "respect our elders," there's a reason that the Bible says, "Fathers, provoke not your children" (Colossians 3:21). It matters to God how parents treat their kids.

* * *

Never humiliate your teens.

* * *

Failure to respect your teens can quickly result in degradation of their self-respect. Since all parents care about their children's behavior, they must also care about their level of self-respect. **Never humiliate your teens.**

You can humiliate them by yelling at them in public, mistreating them in front of their friends, showing physical hostility in front of others, or even calling them names. Get your point across, but do it in private and with respect.

Concerning the "praising in public" part of this motto, teens are often hurt and offended by parents' praising in public if they don't also compliment them in private. They perceive that behavior to be flaunting for others but not genuine encouragement for them. This provokes teens to reject the compliments altogether. **There must be a healthy balance of praising in public and in private, but correcting only in private.**

Remember: Respect their reputation in order to promote their self-respect. Their self-respect will grant you a smoother parent-teen relationship as well as better conduct from your teens.

Productive Mind Games

"You're ugly, and you're stupid, and you're selfish, and you're unkind!" [Silence]

"And you still haven't changed your attitude! And you're not even sorry." [More silence]

"You are just like your daddy," the mother yelled, this time with the sound of her voice choking back tears.

"Just go, just go!!! Go get in the d*mn car and let's get the h*ll out of here!"

Wow. What a heartbreaking scene to witness while standing in line for a dressing room at the mall! After the little girl (who appeared to be 10-13 years old) ran out of the dressing room, I (Kirstie) could hear the sound of the mother emotionally breaking down in the dressing room, crying alone.

Three different emotions flooded my heart at once: 1) hurt for the little girl, 2) anger over the mother's heartlessness, and 3) compassion for the mother's obvious brokenness. Her life's frustration clearly extended far beyond whatever foolish mistakes her daughter had made at the mall that day.

How is a young girl supposed to process such piercing words like these? No apology can truly erase the damage done to her self-image.

Imagine what anyone, and especially a young girl, would think of herself after this? With this kind of treatment happening in a mall dressing room, we can safely assume that it wasn't the first time and wouldn't be the last time that this mother degrades her daughter.

Typically, people say that, if no one else thinks you are beautiful, smart, and have potential, it's your mom. But if your very own mother talks to you like this, what are you to think? If you don't believe her after the first verbal attack, you will believe her eventually. Misused "mind games," as we call it in this subsection, reap painful results that last far beyond adolescent years. But what if you use mind games productively?

"You are so mature for your age"; "You're wise beyond your years"; "You're an exceptional person, very different from the rest of the kids your age." Imagine growing up hearing words like these repeatedly.

Eventually, when it's time to make decisions, these words will resurface in your mind. In fact, you'll find messages like these resounding in your subconscious when considering succumbing to negative temptation: "Man, I'm too wise and mature to do this... I can't. People like me don't do stuff like that."

Although this might sound a bit unrealistic to you, this depiction accurately illustrates our experience growing up. A major reason that our parents constantly received compliments about how well-behaved their five children were is that they convinced each of us that we were smarter, wiser, and more mature than what we were. These are beneficial mind games!

Whether they truly believed we were exceptional kids or not, we don't know. But they surely did make us think so! They accomplished this through repetition and sincerity (not sarcasm). They said it often, and they looked us in the eyes and smiled.

When we were very young, we behaved so well in public that people would approach our parents in restaurants, placing money in our father's hand! "Wow! These are the best behaved kids I've ever seen! How did you get all five of them to be so well-behaved?" they would ask.

Don't be fooled though: they didn't just *tell* us that we were wise, mature, and exceptional, but they *treated* us as if we exemplified all of these qualities. In other words, they treated us with respect.

Even when we made mistakes, as kids do, they did not treat us like criminals. They also never called us any profane or derogatory names.

Because we truly believed that they respected us, it was easier for us to respect them and to desire to live up to who they believed us to be.

It was not fear of punishment that caused us to behave well: our positive behavior flowed from our identity as mature, responsible, wise children of God. Our parents made us believe that we were above the stereotype of others our age. They made us feel like human beings and not just kids, so we strived to behave like responsible individuals and not just the average teenagers.

We can remember being around other adults who made us feel small—like our opinions and ideas didn't matter. They clearly communicated through their words and attitudes that they believed all young people were the same. They left no room for us to be "good kids."

Sometimes, we felt the need to prove ourselves in order to break out of the box that they put us in verbally. We noticed a difference in their expectations for our behavior, and we preferred to receive respect and to be trusted to give it in return.

In those instances, we could feel how easy it was for the average teen to fall into stereotypical behavior. They were treated like that negative behavior was actually the standard!

The negative phases that teenagers tend to go through are typically expected and accepted as normal and inevitable. "All teenagers are on social media 24-7," and "all of you guys have short attention spans." "All teenagers go through this rebellious phase where they don't want to listen to anyone or do anything productive." "Teenagers never listen!" "All teenage boys think about is SEX." "Teens are selfish, irresponsible, and immature."

Although these statements are true for many adolescents, it's simply not true for everyone. It could be true for even fewer teenagers if words were used more intentionally and effectively.

Please pay attention to what you're doing to the mindset of youth with your words! They can sense your perspective of them, even if you don't verbalize negative labels directly. Consider eradicating all negative stereotypes of teens, such as the following:

Teenagers are always...
- Rebellious
- Out-of-control
- Lazy
- Irresponsible
- Partying wildly
- Poor decision-makers
- Troublemakers
- Immature/childish
- Hooligans
- Untrustworthy
- Sexually promiscuous
- Mischievous
- Liars
- Foolish
- Profane (cursing a lot!)
- Nonchalant

- Obsessed with technology
- Disrespectful
- Rude (lacking manners or home-training)
- Crime-prone
- Ignorant
- Reckless
- Binge-drinkers
- Obnoxious

Teens have the potential to be amazing, upstanding citizens who are respectful, articulate, responsible, insightful, mature, moral individuals. Understand that, in decades past, teenagers were married, caring for their families, and living as responsible young adults. It used to be the norm that they learned how to do life independently at an early age and work like adults.

Contrarily, adolescents are expected to be irresponsible in today's society. Parents don't commonly raise the standard because they expect foolish behavior from teens, and American society nurtures immaturity and irresponsibility in this age bracket.

Likewise, maturity and responsibility can be taught. Instead of doing the easier thing—retreating to the stereotypes and "calling it like you see it"—exercise the more productive practice of using mind games to convince them that they are the exceptional people that you know they can be. Accordingly, provide the training they need to learn the responsibility that supports the mindset you are instilling.

The Prophetic Nature of Your Words

Speaking Their Destiny

"Y ou girls are going to be some great event planners one day," said Dad. Our thoughts were something like, "Huh? All we do is plan sleepovers. How would he know if we're good at event planning? We don't even have an interest in doing that."

It is true that our sleepovers were very skillfully planned, though. We started planning months in advance and created full schedules for the nights and subsequent mornings, including time brackets for mealtimes, specific activities, movies, and girl talk.

We created our own games that we still use today for various youth group activities! And, what do you know? Our first job right after college graduation was as youth event coordinators for Word of Faith Family Worship Cathedral!

The reason we were offered the position is that we voluntarily planned a large youth conference annually, starting in our sophomore year of college. This ticketed event began with 500 students in attendance, and by the fourth year, there were 1,300 in attendance!

Dad was right after all: we were gifted to plan events, and we actually loved it!

It's amazing how words from parents can help to shape your reality.

When our brother was in middle school, our mom would sometimes hear him sing just a little here and there, and she would say, "Dale can really sing! He has a beautiful voice!—Just watch! He is really going to be singing one day."

The rest of us would respond, "No he can't! He doesn't even sing!" (At this time, three of us were in the choir, and he was not in that number.)

He soon began to say, "One day I'm going to join the teen choir." Still doubtful that he had the talent or true desire, his sisters sarcastically responded, "Yeah, right!"

Despite our negativity, our mom kept believing in him and encouraging him. When he came of age, he immediately joined the teen choir. He later became the tenor section leader and the lead male soloist on the worship team!

All of his teenage years, he sang around the house all the time, even creating short, catchy songs, almost like jingles. Annoyed, all of his siblings would scream phrases like this: "Shut up, Dale!" "Be quiet!" "You are getting on my nerves!"

His strong voice echoed throughout the house, especially when we moved into a home covered with wooden floors!

Meanwhile, our mother was always affirming his musical gift: "Boy, you are so talented!" "Dale, you can sing!" "Wow, that song could be a hit!" "You're really going to be amazing one day!" She would even sing his little jingles with him.

She definitely spoke his gift into existence. As a college student, he was actively writing songs, playing guitar, and touching thousands of people with his music! It is now evident to many that he has an amazing gift, and finally we've all stopped telling him to shut up. 😊

Another example of our parents' powerful encouragement involved our poetry-writing during our early teen years. Our parents always spoke highly of it, even more than what we originally thought it deserved. They made us feel so encouraged when we shared our poetry that we practically ran to meet them with every new poem! They pumped us up so much that we even shared it publicly and won an award.

One day, our mother asked us if we ever thought about writing songs. We never had. She said, "You girls do such an amazing job with poetry, and you can sing well. I bet you can write songs too. Songs are basically poems set to music."

After that day, we both tried writing songs and ended up trading poetry-writing altogether for songwriting. If it had not been for the words from Mom, we might never have begun writing music.

It's interesting to note how you can speak your teen's destiny

● ● ●

Whatever is repeated will stick, whether positive or negative.

● ● ●

into existence, in the overall direction of their careers and even in the seemingly small things concerning their character, personality, or talents.

Ever since we were young children, our sister Neiel always took initiative to care for her siblings when we were sick or hurting, particularly our brother. She would even let him sleep in the bed with her sometimes when he had a stomachache.

Noticing these instances, our parents began to reinforce that behavior with their words. They would say: "Wow, Neiel is a nurturer! She has a very nurturing and motherly spirit."

She currently has three young children of her own and is one of the best mothers we know! It is extremely rare to find young mothers (Neiel is married, by the way. 😊) who have as much wisdom and grace as she does. Her heart concerning motherhood is very inspiring, and we pray to one day be as passionate about it as she is when we become mothers.

Isn't it powerful to realize that you can use words to shape your teen's destiny in numerous aspects?!

These are just a few examples of how our parents spoke various components of our destinies, gifts, and personalities into existence; but honestly, we could write a whole book solely on all of the words of affirmation that our parents spoke into our lives that helped develop us into who we are today. You could call it prophecy because it all came true!

Also note that our parents didn't speak these "prophecies" to us only once, and it is no coincidence that we remember them. They repeated the affirmations. Repetition is key to using words to mold your teen's mindset. Without repetition, the positive statements won't stick. **Whatever is repeated will stick, whether positive or negative.**

Unfortunately, much of the detriment to families in today's society is due to all of the negative words that are repeated more than the positive. Every time kids are told they're the "bad child" or that they're "just like their father," when that has a negative connotation, their minds are molded in a shape that isn't befitting of who you (or God) desire for them to become. It actually takes about 10 positive statements to counteract the effects of just one negative one.

Therefore, be intentional to consistently encourage your teens and nurture every gift you find.

Name to Reality

It's fascinating to see the effects of what you repeatedly call your children, including what you name them. If you already have children you've named, what's done is done. If you realize that the meaning of your kids' names is not what you desire to prove true for their lives, speak other positive words to them that align with their destinies.

If you plan to have children in the future, pay close attention to this subsection regarding the realistic connection between names and destiny.

Noah, a fairly well known man recorded in the Bible, had an interesting prophecy over his life via his name. Noah is known for building the famous ark, which preserved life on Earth by saving only Noah's family and various animal species. All else perished in the Great Flood, which was sent to destroy every other living thing on Earth.

Noah is known to be a savior of some sort, since he preserved the human race and animal life from extinction. He, the only righteous leader living at that time, did this out of his obedience to God. He was notably moral and noble, and the Bible says that he "found grace in the sight of the Lord" (Genesis 6:8).

After the flood, he and his family were charged with repopulating the earth. What a task! The great part about all that he endured was that there was more peace in the earth and less violence after the flood. (The destruction of mankind was because of the violence and wickedness of people *before* the flood.)

Of no coincidence, at Noah's birth, his father, Lamech, named him saying, "This one will give us a break from the hard work of farming the ground…" (Genesis 5:29 MSG). His name means "rest, comfort." Noah definitely brought quite a break from laboring in the fields!

Jacob is another biblical example of someone living the meaning of his name. Jacob was a blessed man who was the chosen heir of God's promises given to Abraham—to bless all the nations of the earth through him and multiply his descendants like the stars in the sky and like the sand on the seashore.

Although Jacob would receive many blessings, he would also struggle with a particular flaw in alignment with the name his parents gave him. He tricked Esau, his older twin, into selling him his birthright as the eldest son.

Also, because his father was blind, Jacob was able to convince his dad that he was Esau, in order to steal the blessing from his twin. To no surprise, Jacob's name means "deceiver!" Later, God changed his name to Israel, meaning "God will prevail" because he struggled with God and men and was victorious. His new name also proved true as is evident in his great legacy.

Interestingly enough, our first names, Kirstie and Kristie, mean the same thing and so do our middle names, Alexandra and Alexis. Notice that Kirstie and Kristie are not the same name. You switch the letters *r* and *i* to create different names with different pronunciations. (We have to clarify because even our doctor's office mistook one of our records for duplicates!) Our first names both mean "anointed Christian," and our middle names both mean "helper of mankind."

Although we have all of the same interests, favorite foods, values, and passions, our personalities are different. Nevertheless, our destinies align in unmistakable ways. Our careers and life goals beautifully intersect, as we are a God-breathed team in many endeavors, serving God and helping people.

Two people with different names that mean the same thing—

it makes perfect sense! Concerning the reality of our names, we are both passionate about Jesus Christ—anointed Christians—, and we both are very driven to help mankind, as we have been for many years. From teaching Sunday school classes to planning youth conferences to creating and facilitating mentoring programs to writing self-help books, we continue to extend our hearts and hands to help mankind.

It is definitely worthwhile to be intentional about what you name your children, considering something more than how "pretty" or "cute" the name sounds. Whatever qualities you desire to see as overarching themes in your children's lives, consider those in the naming process.

Using Positive Confessions

There is great power in repeating the same positive statements to your teens regularly and even having them repeat the statements after you (call and response) sometimes. It's an excellent way to drill key perspectives into their minds and ensure they never forget them. They will likely carry those practices with them and repeat your words to their friends and even to their own kids one day.

When our father dropped us off at elementary school, he would playfully yell out of the car "Get that lesson!" We laughed and looked around to see if any of the other kids heard him, hoping that he hadn't embarrassed us. 😳

Other than the occasional embarrassment, we enjoyed the laugh that started our morning in a lighthearted fashion and emphasized the value of education (although we weren't thinking about that part at the time, haha). We were both on the honor roll every year of elementary school, so we actually did "get that lesson!" We later realized that this confession was generational, passing from our grandmother, to our father, to us.

Also, our father used to wake us up every morning shouting, "How are you feeling this morning?!" and expecting us to respond with one specific word, spoken one particular way—

"GRRREAT!" If we mumbled "okay," "good," or "fine," he would repeat the question again and again until we enthusiastically responded "GRRREAT!!!"

This was a joyful, energetic way to wake us up every day. It taught us to have a positive attitude, even in the morning. We learned to wake up each morning with great expectations for the day. This confession continued generationally as well, passing from our grandfather, to our father, to us.

In our house, it wasn't normal to walk around silent and pouting in the morning, partially because of this simple routine with our father. When we saw others appearing angry in the morning, excusing their attitude with, "I'm not a morning person," we realized the power in what we had learned at home. This distinguished us from the average person in the morning.

What also impacted our perspective about each day was the scripture that both of our parents often stated upon waking up— "This is the day that the Lord has made, and I will rejoice and be [exceedingly] glad in it!" (Psalm 118:24) This verse taught us to be grateful for each day, viewing it as a blessing from God, no matter how tired our bodies felt.

Another example of a memorable verbal ritual was our mother's singing. In the morning, when our mom woke us up, she often sang this corny song that said, "Rise and shine and give God the glory!" To this day, we aren't sure if she created that song, or if it was an established song.

Having heard her sing this numerous times, we have found ourselves singing this same tune to wake up our friends at sleepovers, to wake up one another, and even to wake up teenagers on various youth retreats for mentoring or team building. It continues to bring laughs and smiles to the morning every time.

Additionally, every morning as our mom drove us to elementary school, she recited this long confession and had us repeat each line after her: "I'm the head and not the tail. I'm above only and not beneath. I'm a lender and not a borrower. I will do my best and trust God to do the rest!"

● ● ●

*I*ntentionally repeat *what you want to* see.

● ● ●

Keep in mind that the shorter the confession, the more likely your kids are to remember it. Like we said, that confession was a long one, so what's written above is the only part we remember. Haha!

The line "Do your best and trust God to do the rest" is what really stuck out above everything else. After hearing that everyday throughout elementary school, we ended up using it as a life motto and repeating it when we do inspirational speaking, when we pray, and when we write.

What power lies in words by simply confessing with your mouth exactly what you desire to see in your life and in the lives of your children! Remember that the words of parents to their kids hold great power and should be used wisely.

Intentionally *repeat* what you want to *see*.

Affirmation

What You *Don't* Say

Have you ever heard that when people's bodies are deficient in certain nutrients, they begin to have cravings, often for junk foods that contain some of that nutrient? For example, your body might need calcium, and you begin craving ice cream. Or you might be dehydrated, and you crave a coke.

Emotional cravings work similarly, although the consequences of bad substitutes are far worse than fat from junk food.

This is why your compliments and words of affirmation matter. When you fail to tell your teens things like "Good job," "I'm proud of you," "You're beautiful/handsome," and "You're so talented," they become emotionally starved and seek those words from others.

The consequences are quite diverse, including, but certainly not limited to, vulnerability to involvement in unhealthy romantic or sexual relationships. **Voids often lead people to unhealthy behavior because they tend to use what's most convenient, rather than what's best, to fill those voids.**

For example, a teenage girl who never heard words like, "You're special," "You're beautiful," "You're valuable," "I love you" from her father will likely be more susceptible to flattery by the first charming boy.

He can mistreat her, even abuse her, and she will probably stick around so that she can occasionally hear those endearing words again. That way, she can at least feel special sometimes.

Because she doesn't understand her worth and this boy is her main source

● ● ●

Voids often lead people to unhealthy behavior because they tend to use what's most convenient, rather than what's best, to fill those voids.

● ● ●

● ● ●

A hug can say what your words cannot or should not sometimes.

● ● ●

of affection, she is vulnerable. She will likely feel that, where he goes, so goes her validation. And she'll believe that without him, she is alone. So she'll bury the bad stuff and keep coming back.

Not only are words of affirmation vital, but also words of comfort. When a child has fallen off of his/her bike, a simple kiss and "It's gonna be okay" or "You're all right (with a comforting smile)" can seem to erase the pain. At any age, when your kids need comfort because of loss or hurt, your words are invaluable.

Drenched with pain, these words seeped from the lips of an emotionally broken college student: "When my real [biological] father passed, my step-dad didn't even say anything to me."

Wow! When she needed words of comfort from her stepfather, his silence wounded her deeply. He was probably afraid of saying the wrong thing, unable to find the right words, or maybe even unsure if she wanted to hear anything from him at all.

Although words may be hard to find at times, please remember that what you *don't* say also matters.

Your silence can communicate messages of emotional abandonment when: your child fails miserably on an academic project that she worked on tirelessly; your son loses his most important football game of the year; your daughter experiences a painful break-up after a 2-year relationship; or when your son experiences the "premature" death of one of his classmates.

We are not saying to start blabbing as soon as you find out something bad happened. But we are saying that your response, or lack thereof, makes a difference.

Keep in mind that you can also communicate through body language. **A hug can say what your words cannot or should not sometimes.**

When a teenage boy just endured the most humiliating,

scary, and painful moment of his life, he called his father. As an adult, he remembered the impact of his father's response.

His father hurried to pick him up and took him to one of his favorite places to eat. His dad then simply sat with him while he cried incessantly. His father's presence and compassion meant the world to him. When he composed himself after about two hours, his father encouraged him.

In this scenario, you must consider that the place his father picked him up from was jail. His dad could have scolded him, condemned him, and told him what an idiot he was for getting himself caught up in that situation. Instead, he empathized with him and uplifted him.

His son expressed that, on this night, his dad was really a father to him. He carried that moment in his heart as a treasure, a token of his father's love truly proven.

You don't have to create a whole speech for your teens in their hard times because sometimes that can be overbearing. Show them your compassion through a hug, prayer, and simple phrases like these: "I'm so sorry to hear that." "I'll be praying for you." "I'm here for you." "Just let me know if there's anything I can do to help."

It's also important to acknowledge the weight of the issue, validating your teen's feelings by saying phrases like, "Wow, I know it hurts…" "Woah, that's big," or "Mmm, I feel you."

Although these concise phrases seem basic, they can make a big difference. If you don't respond at all in an attempt to avoid "getting in their business" or in an effort to remain upbeat, your teen might feel like you don't care. A simple phone call or text message can mean more than you know.

Lastly, what you *don't* say that is quite damaging is what has been termed "the silent treatment." Have you ever hurt someone, disappointed him, or even angered a person so much that he/she stopped speaking to you altogether? Consider how that made you feel.

"The silent treatment" can be just as hurtful as what you do say. Your teens can feel condemned, isolated, and like the scum of the earth if you refuse to speak to them.

Despite what they've done, extended periods of nonexistent verbal communication are unhealthy. Notice we specified "verbal" communication. You're still communicating negativity through the look of disdain in your eyes and through the resentful vibes that you emit.

Be mindful that some situations might seem small to you but be quite memorable for your teens. So always remember to say something when it counts. Make sure that your teens know that you are there for them and cheering them on through the ups and downs.

The Small Things Matter!

The following text message was sent during a time of serious strain upon a mother-daughter relationship:

> My mom just called me, and we talked for a while, and laughed a little bit. Then before she got off the phone she said, "I love you." To some people, that isn't a big deal… But it's an enormous deal for me!!! I don't know when the last time she said those words to me was… I mean, I never doubted her love for me, but hearing her say it and mean it, was like an out-of-body experience for me… I didn't know 3 words could affect me like it just did. God did ALL of that!!!

You'd be surprised how much the small things matter to your teens. They crave encouragement and compliments, even when you think it's too small to make a difference.

During a conversation with a teenager, I (Kirstie) was reminded of the importance of the little things… Although she said that her parents often hurt her with their words, she thought it was significant to tell me that her dad told her she did a good job vacuuming the carpet. "That made me feel good," she sweetly commented.

Another example of a kid who craved the seemingly small

things from her parents was Sharon. Sharon is a young adult who has numerous unresolved issues with her father from her childhood. These issues continue to impact her life as a married

The small sacrifices are the investments for a big, priceless return.

woman with two kids of her own. Her father was highly abusive to her, verbally and physically, ever since she can remember.

When asked what her dad could do to make her feel more loved and appreciated, she simply replied that she would like for him to just call and tell her [how much he loves and appreciates her]. "That's all he has to do, and I feel like I would melt," she said. I'm sure many would somberly and wholeheartedly agree with that. So-called "small" things matter.

Sometimes, our dad sends us encouraging text messages or even funny pictures with captions that make us fall out laughing, and every text is precious to us. It makes us feel really special because he was thinking of us.

Every time that our mom does the smallest favor for us with a big smile, saying, "My pleasure," it warms our hearts and makes us feel truly loved. The fact that she is happy to do nice things for us, no matter how big or small… It's no hassle, no imposition, and no running tab to repay later.

Think about it—simple acts of kindness and thoughtfulness, especially involving your positive words, can make a big difference in the self-image of your teens and in the health of your relationship with them. **The small sacrifices are the investments for a big, priceless return.**

Parent Personalities

What if verbalizing your feelings to your teens, whether positive or negative, is difficult for you because your personality is not outgoing or expressive? What if you are naturally reserved, quiet, or shy?

Well, your kids *still* need your affirmation! Nevertheless, don't be discouraged. Our dad has always claimed to be naturally shy, even though he speaks to crowds of thousands. We've come to realize that he was telling the truth!

Our mom is the outgoing one who tackles uncomfortable topics with ease and who voices her feelings often. Our dad, however, expresses himself differently.

If the topic is uncomfortable, sometimes he tells Mom how he feels, and she relays his sentiments to us. Or he might just communicate his perspective in a more subtle way.

But even though he isn't typically emotional or expressive, he never omits affirmation. If we do something noteworthy, he often tells us how excellent it was, how we did such an exceptional job, and how he greatly enjoyed it. He raves about it so eloquently that it sounds even better than it actually was!

When we are leaving the dinner table with the family and he is hugging us goodbye, he will reiterate his encouragement followed by, "I'm so proud of you."

He also sends his affirmations through text messages, as we mentioned above. And he's even written each of his children encouraging letters that he's given us by hand.

Even if we haven't done anything recently that is extraordinary, he will brag about us to others in our presence. And he regularly compliments us on little things like how stylish our outfit is or how beautiful our hair looks.

Whether it's a small verbal compliment, an encouraging text message, an uplifting letter, a "Great job today," or an "I'm so proud of you," every word—verbal, written, typed, elaborate, or simple—warms our hearts, builds our self-confidence, and means the world to us.

Regardless of your personality type, do what you can to communicate uplifting words to your teens.

Energy for the Soul

How heartbreaking to hear that a young man wanted to become a doctor, but his dad told him, "That is for smart people, and just face it—those kinds of genes don't exactly run in our family. Apply for something practical that you can actually do, and gain a steady paycheck. We don't have the money to send you to a fancy medical school anyway."

What about right after a student finishes singing in a recital when her parents just give a thumbs-up, say, "That was nice," and proceed to discuss the family's dinner plans?

● ● ●

Sometimes, that encouragement serves as the propeller for people's gifts, thrusting them forward with energy and confidence.

● ● ●

Effectively communicating your affirmation matters.

There are numerous individuals that live miserable lives, working towards nothing but a paycheck. Many are scared to share their dreams with anyone for fear of being criticized or judged. Some believe that dreams are only relevant while sleeping.

Who will draw out the gifts that your teens might not realize they have? Who will liberate them to pursue the passions and goals that are in their hearts, letting them know that it is possible?

Often, after people, regardless of age, perform, create something, make a kind gesture, or step out of their comfort zone, they are seeking some type of validation. They are hoping that someone will confirm that they have just done well. **Sometimes, that encouragement serves as the propeller for people's gifts, thrusting them forward with energy and confidence.**

Our parents have always told us, "You can do anything you put your mind to. Whatever you choose, you can become the best in that field! You are more than able!"

As we previously mentioned, they first encouraged us with our childhood poetry, and we gained the confidence to sharpen our writing skills. We didn't even think our poetry was very good until they responded like, "Oh my goodness! That is

> • • •
>
> *Your encouragement creates an environment where limitations don't exist.*
>
> • • •

fantastic! So much wisdom! Wow! You sound like you're well beyond your years. You should read this to others. This is truly excellent!"

Their words replayed in our minds over and over again, and we kept writing. Who knew that we'd one day become authors of books?!

Parents, when your child presents papers, projects, artwork, and more, make sure to applaud him/her like it's the greatest work you've ever seen! It builds kids' confidence at a young age and breeds excitement in them to share their creations throughout life.

Naturally, people are apprehensive about showing things they have created, whether songs, poems, art, designs, business ideas, or goals. Without the encouragement of parents as they're growing, teens can develop very low self-confidence and might be afraid of exposing and pursuing their aspirations.

Be careful to never stifle creativity in your kids. Some of the greatest inventions that exist today were called stupid by someone at some point. Don't let that person be you!

The same abstract art that one person thinks is simple, boring, and "like it could have been done by a 3-year-old," someone somewhere is paying thousands of dollars to own and place in his multi-million dollar home!

Be determined not to be a dream-crusher, even if you're not sure what your child's dream is yet. Whatever your kid produces from his/her creativity, as long as it's not immoral, should be celebrated! Your teens should always know they have your support.

Your encouragement creates an environment where limitations don't exist. You liberate your teens to be anything and do anything when you serve as their personal cheerleader before anyone else has the opportunity to tell them they "can't."

Our parents simply encouraged our creativity and our passions that they saw naturally arising. They cultivated an atmosphere of freedom and confidence so that we could develop into driven, happy, creative people.

They did this through singing our praises with great enthusiasm every time we used our gifts to create something or present some talent. **Whatever you want to see more of in your teens, encourage that! Let your words build wings for them to fly.**

● ● ●

Whatever you want to see more of in your teens, encourage that! Let your words build wings for them to fly.

● ● ●

How NOT to Communicate

Words Worth Regretting

Although most parents would nearly lose their minds hearing that their child was physically attacked at school, they often fail to realize this: **The damage that you do with your words has far more long-lasting effects than any physical beating your teen could receive at school or elsewhere.**

An intense example is that of John Ramirez, a former Satanist who later became a Christian. The root of his hatred, hardness of heart, and evil intentions was emotional pain from his father. Not only was John's father often absent, but also when his dad was home, he destroyed his son's morale through his harsh, piercing words.

Because his own father had abandoned him emotionally, and many times even physically, when presented with the idea, John turned to Satan as his "father."

One of the many stories from his childhood that led to his downward spiral is in the following excerpt from his book, *Out of the Devil's Cauldron*:

> I never knew who my father really was [even though John lived with his father!] and wondered if he even liked us, but I couldn't figure out why not. I saw other boys with their fathers going to the park, hitting a ball, playing catch, talking about sports. Those fathers would talk enthusiastically with them, pat them on the back, and walk along with their sons, sharing a good laugh. I

The damage that you do with your words has far more long-lasting effects than any physical beating your teen could receive at school or elsewhere.

yearned for that kind of relationship, but no matter what I tried, he'd just push me away and call me "stupid." Some words are shattering to a child, and stupid is certainly one of them... He seemed to go out of his way to discourage my brothers and me, to criticize us and talk to us in a condescending tone. We were never good enough to make him happy (Ramirez, Pp. 21-22).

The negative words of John's father led him to a very dark place...

What a shame it is when parents allow their personal frustrations to provoke them to emotionally wound their children!

Of course, there are two sides to every story. We understand that teens often provoke their parents by unruly behavior, negative attitudes, and annoying tendencies.

We also understand that parents are people, too! As humans, we tend to subconsciously project our issues upon others, most commonly those closest to us.

We all know that, even when we see people cursing out their waiter, they're reacting to more than just the petty incident at the restaurant—they're subconsciously projecting their own issues onto the poor server who just made a mistake!

The problem is that you just cannot afford to damage your teens with your words.

Avoid allowing your own frustrations to influence the way you treat your teens. Realistically, it's challenging to keep your kids from feeling the effects of your bad days, and sometimes nearly impossible. But don't punish them because of your issues. Take a moment to compose yourself, if you need to.

Also, try explaining to them that you're under pressure and that they're not the cause of your frustration. For example, "Baby, I'm sorry for my tone. It's really not you: it's me. Mommie's/Daddy's going through a rough time right now." **You can't keep the fights of life from coming, but you can keep your teens from being in the boxing ring with you!**

Teens already hear negative words from peers and even

some teachers. Home should be the safe place where they are affirmed, nurtured, and grounded on a firm foundation.

Therefore, of all the regrets you could have in life, don't make your words to your teens one of them.

Be Careful with Your Questions

"Your lips look different... You haven't been smoking anything, have you?"

"You sure have been experiencing stomach aches frequently these days, and it's not even your period yet... Are you pregnant?"

"I smell alcohol on you. Have you been drinking?!"

Part of quality parenting is awareness of your teen's personal life, including relationships, academics, and spirituality. One of the key tools in acquiring this information is inquiry. However, there is a *way* to ask questions to your teens, and there is a way NOT to ask...

Always remember that asking questions is necessary, but making negative assumptions and accusations is not.

You will be surprised what a difference it makes in your relationship with your teens when you assume the best about them! Of course, you must take into consideration individuals' differences: if your teen has a history of certain types of behavior, you should gently ask him/her important questions directly. Don't automatically assume, yell the question, or fuss.

For example, if your teenager has a history of smoking marijuana, and you smell smoke on him, you could try asking something like this: "Hey Jay, glad to see you made it home safely. Uhh, something smells like marijuana... Were you around some other kids smoking tonight? Or did you make a mistake with this again?"

Always hope and pray for the best, and grant them

Always remember that asking questions is necessary, but making negative assumptions and accusations is not.

the right to change at any point. If you don't, you will nail them to their past mistakes and consequently create a negative label, whether intentionally or unintentionally. If you know that your teen does not have a history of certain negative behavior, always assume the best, unless you have *concrete* evidence to prove otherwise.

For example, because we never smoked anything, if we came home smelling like marijuana, our parents would not ask if we'd been smoking.

They might playfully ask something like, "Ooo, your jacket smells like weed. Where have you girls been?" Surely enough, in a situation like this, we were returning from our college's parking deck where a couple of students were smoking marijuana right next to our car.

Our parents could still discover the same information without making us feel like they thought we were hooligans prone to anything troublesome.

It's a dangerous thing for teens to feel like their parents don't think anything is beneath them, like nothing is too far-fetched for them to be involved in. Remember, they need to know you think highly of them so that they will think highly of themselves. This approach gives them higher standards to live up to.

"My mom has asked me if I was pregnant many times... Just because I have big breasts and a big butt, and I have an older boyfriend does not mean I am sleeping around. It cuts my heart deeply every time she accuses me with that question."

After talking with this particular young lady, we were even more keenly aware of what a big deal simple questions can be. It's understandable that her mother would get concerned sometimes and want to put her mind at ease, being reassured that her daughter isn't pregnant.

The real question is, do you want to know so badly that it's worth straining your parent-teen relationship? In a case like this, the mother should've welcomed her daughter to discuss her dating relationship and habits with her so that she could remain abreast of what was going on in her daughter's life.

When her daughter returned home from dates, she should've asked, "Hey sweetie! How was your date? I hope you two had a nice time. What did you guys do?" Or even more directly, "Hey! How was your date? How are you two doing with your sexual boundaries?" (Of course, only one question at a time... Listen well and then ask the next one.)

Simple, friendly questions along the way can help to prevent the need for questions like, "Are you pregnant?"

Don't wait until you want to know the big stuff before you start asking the little things. When you ask the little things along the way, it's easier for your questions to remain casual. These questions also create accountability for your teens, as we discuss in the "Friend or Parent" chapter.

Sometimes, parents make the mistake of giving little to no attention unless something bad happens. In contrast, you should remain involved throughout the journey. **The more light-hearted questions you ask along the way, the fewer hurtful surprises you'll find.**

You shouldn't wait until the girl becomes your son's girlfriend before you know her. You should take interest in your teens' friends to the extent that, if they begin a dating relationship, you already know the girl or guy. You can do this by hosting your teen's gatherings at your house and chatting with their friends a bit every now and then. You can even invite your teen's closest friends to family dinner sometimes.

It's unwise to wait until your teen is in love before you care to know what girl/boy your child is interested in. It's appropriate to ask, "Hey honey, who's that girl? She seems nice. Tell me about her... 😊 What is she like? [He responds.] Oh okay, you two becoming pretty good friends?"

Be careful of blatantly voicing negative opinions of your teens' friends or romantic interests, especially if you know that your child is already pretty attached to the person. You don't want your teen to start defending his/her friend instead of sincerely hearing and receiving your concerns.

If you want your teens to recognize your perspective about a friend, ask them questions that cause them to evaluate the person and come to the conclusions themselves.

> ● ● ●
>
> *People don't do what you nag them to do: they do what you encourage them to do.*
>
> ● ● ●

For example, "Sally seems sweet... When you're around her, does she inspire you to be a better person? What do you feel like Sally adds to you as a person? Does she share your values?"

Questions are powerful tools. Ask the right questions the right way, and you'll see better results.

No Nagging Necessary

Have you ever felt like a person tells you much more negative stuff about you than positive? Like they always have something bad to say, fussing about what you do wrong instead of applauding what you actually do right? Not very encouraging, is it?

"Hello?! What are y'all in here doing? I told you to wash these dishes! Get your butts up right now and clean this kitchen! You all need to stop watching so much television and get up and be productive! Don't be lazy bums!"

It's safe to assume that every child has been annoyed by parental nagging. Sometimes so much so that kids dread their parents' arrival back home. What if this same concept causes resentment and possibly rebellion in the teen when the matter does not involve household chores, but rather more important life decisions?

Often, our father has said, **"People don't do what you nag them to do: they do what you encourage them to do."** This statement proves true in every area of life, and it is particularly useful with your children as they develop.

When your teens feel that the good things they do are acknowledged, and they won't be a permanent screw-up in your eyes, they tend to work harder to please you. Also, people respond better to positive language than negative language in general, even if the bottom line is the same. Always consider how you can communicate more positively.

When we were 15 years old, we began teaching a Sunday school class along with our older sister, Neiel. At first, all three of us were extremely shy and nervous, but we felt we should do it, so we did. We taught 14-18-year-old young ladies, meaning that we were actually younger than some of the students we taught! Neiel was 18 at the time.

For the first few months, it was difficult, but it was going amazingly well. We were creating memorable visuals, bringing props, and packing the class with energy and innovative ideas that kept lessons engaging and substantive. It was enough to keep young people wide awake early in the morning!

After a few months, we became discouraged, feeling like we were running out of ideas. And after ample discussion among the three of us, we informed our parents that we would like to quit. In a situation like this, most parents would have commanded, "Finish what you started! You will not quit! I didn't raise any quitters!" On the contrary, our father remained calm and simply encouraged us.

He kept the situation light-hearted, laughing at our descriptions such as, "We used to have cool examples, like peeling back the layers of a rotten onion and a fresh one to demonstrate getting to the core of who you really are, but now we're all out of ideas!"

He explained that it was great training ground for us to develop as effective communicators in front of audiences. He also told us that our discouragement was natural at that point in our journey. Our dad validated our feelings, but informed us that they were only temporary. He gently challenged us saying, "Why don't you girls stick it out for another six months, and if you still want to quit by then, go ahead." What wisdom!

Sure enough, by the end of those six months, we had grown

tremendously and matured through that dry, difficult season. Notice that no nagging was necessary to accomplish the goal. If he had become frustrated with us and forced us to continue, we probably would have done so but with discouragement and anger, without as much effort. His positive approach was much more beneficial.

Concerning things like chores or homework, it's probably safe to say that all parents nag their kids. For some reason, teens tend to have a natural disgust for responsibility. Compared with video games, TV, sports, talking on the phone, going to the mall, and hanging out with friends, work easily falls to the bottom of the priority list.

They simply don't *feel* like it most of the time. It seems like a boring waste of time, especially when they're in school and trying to enjoy their free time outside of class.

To be honest, in our household, our sweet, wonderful mother did her share of nagging when it came to cleaning. I'm sure it was difficult not to nag, considering her desire for a clean house amid a seven-person household.

She also encouraged us a lot, which proved to be effective. One time, I (Kirstie) was cleaning the kitchen counters, and she came over to inspect. As she examined the work, she raved over my skills. "Oh wow! Kirstie is amazing at cleaning the counters! She has them just sparkling and shining!" She would say something like this fairly regularly after examining my work with the counters.

I never told her, but that made me feel great! After her first time raving over my work, I began working harder and paying even more attention to detail so that I could please her again and receive more of her praises. It made me feel appreciated and accomplished. I felt like I had just done something important and that my effort mattered.

In middle school, we took a penmanship course, teaching us how to write clearly in cursive. Our parents came into our room raving over my (Kristie's) penmanship assignment. "Kristie's handwriting is so neat, smooth, and pretty! Wow!"—Encouragement like this made me feel like I had the best handwriting in the world, and I continued to work hard in class. After all, I had to uphold my penmanship title of "best cursive"!

It is sad to say that many people are more inclined to emphasize what someone does wrong than what they do well. It is human nature to be negative. Recently, we even chuckled about the study that proved that people talk about $50 lost more than $50 gained! Kids should never be able to recall constant nagging more than the impact of regular encouragement and compliments.

Next time you consider nagging your teen, ask yourself, "When was the last time that I praised him/her?" Think of something that your teen has done right or even just a positive character trait that you can acknowledge. Then, if you have some constructive criticism or instruction to offer, you can proceed to instruct with kindness. We can bet that your teen will then receive it at least a little bit better.

Deciding Your Language

It will not always be easy to filter your words because parents are humans too; but, as mature elders, parents are charged with this great responsibility. This means that, no matter what your teens have done, how angry you are, how disrespected you feel, or how disappointed you have become, you decide to hold on to the hope of who they can be. And you use positive language to draw their potential to the surface.

You will have to bite your tongue many times to ensure you don't say hurtful, degrading things that you might even believe are true! Guess what?—Saying it does not fix it! Confirming in their minds that they are the rebels they think they are only propels them further in that direction.

Look past the behavior to the person, to the potential, to the destiny that God has ordained for that precious life before he/she was even born! Encourage that. Be the one to believe in them before they believe in themselves. Be the one to say, "This is not who you are: You are intelligent, wise, mature, and honorable. You are a child of God. Now, let's start behaving like it."

You want your teens to be able to say of you that you were the one who always encouraged them and saw the best in them, even when they didn't see it in themselves. Be the one to build a firm foundation of confidence in your offspring. With great intentionality and wisdom, you can use the tool of your tongue to do just that, building with "bricks" called "powerful language."

CHAPTER 4
FRIEND OR PARENT

The Beauty of Balance

Alecia: This is not family—it's tyranny! You call this relationship?! It's definitely more of a dictatorship.

Brandon: They're ruining my life, and I hate this prison! I can't wait until I'm 18, and I can move out of here!

Kelley: I can't talk to them about ANYTHING because they're always overreacting! They never listen or even try to understand.

Shawn: My mom lets me do whatever I want. She always says yes—that stupid b****.

Isaac: My parents don't care what I do.

What is the balance between being friendly enough to foster openness and being strict enough to create boundaries for safety and respect?

Have you ever met or seen on the *Maury Show* the parent who smokes weed with his teen and says, "Well, I'd rather he does it in my house so I can supervise"? More commonly, you might know the parent who loves the line "BECAUSE I SAID SO" and whose teens never feel comfortable talking to him about anything. (That might have been you *before* reading this book! Haha!)

Because the purpose of parenting is guiding the child, healthy respect and open communication are both vital. This is why one of the most important keys to healthy parent-teen relationships lies in what we like to call the balance between being friend and parent.

Some parents tell their teens, "I am not your friend: I am your parent." They deem it necessary to draw that line of distinction in order to maintain a certain level of reverence, but does that limitation yield the best product? Is it possible to be both parent and friend?

The answer is undoubtedly YES. Let's look at the best possible example—God. God is father to many children, one to be reverenced, feared, and obeyed. He functions as a father as He provides, protects, guides, and corrects (2 Thessalonians 3:3 and Hebrews 12:5-6). The Bible says, "For the Lord corrects those He loves, just as a father corrects a child in whom he delights."—Proverbs 3:12 NLT

Yet, even God Himself, the Almighty, who created mankind from the dust, gives us the opportunity to know Him as a friend (John 15:14).

Let's take a look at God's relationship with Abraham:

When God planned to destroy Sodom and Gomorrah because of their sin, He discussed His plans with Abraham before He did it. Wow—He's GOD, and He thought enough of His relationship with Abraham to include him in an important decision.

God said, "Shall I hide from Abraham what I am about to do...?" —Gen. 18:17 ESV

So God told Abraham about His plans, and Abraham disagreed. He was adamant about God sparing any righteous people in those cities, if there were any to be found. He went back and forth with God, seemingly negotiating with Him.

Notice the balance Abraham demonstrated. As a friend, he negotiated with God, and God considered his opinion, answered him, and adjusted based upon Abraham's thoughts. But as a child, he was extremely respectful in his approach to "Father" God.

"Then Abraham spoke again, 'Since I have begun, let me speak further to my Lord, even though I am but dust and ashes.'" —Genesis 18:27 NLT

God wasn't obligated to communicate with Abraham before destroying Sodom and Gomorrah. But, God did not want to hide anything from His "friend." The Bible says, "...Abraham believed God, and it was counted to him as righteousness—and he was called a friend of God." —James 2:23 ESV

After sharing His plans with Abraham and hearing Abraham's objections, God could have said, "I didn't ask for your opinion. I'm God, and you're My servant. [Kind of like, "I'm the parent, you're the child"... Sound familiar?] I said I was going to destroy Sodom and Gomorrah, and that's what I'm going to do. Now be quiet."

Instead, God was patient, listened to Abraham, and proved that Abraham's opinion mattered. God searched for the number of righteous people Abraham bargained for in order to spare the city. And when those could not be found, He rescued Abraham's cousin from the town before destroying it.

God and Abraham had real conversation as father and son. And as a result, they developed an intimate relationship.

Remember these words of Jesus: "You are my friends if you do what I command you..." —John 15:14a ESV

As Father God, He corrects us and teaches us self-discipline, patience, and numerous other virtues throughout life. As our friend, He allows us to confide in Him, dialogue with Him, solicit His comfort, and enjoy His company.

Yes, you can be both friend and parent; but the key lies in balance.

The Benefit of "Friend" Status

To clarify, we are not saying that your teens need to call you their friend. We simply refer to "friend" status as the open, nonjudgmental, loving relationship in which your teens actually enjoy being around you, talking with you, and sharing the details of their lives with you.

This kind of relationship requires that they feel comfortable being honest with you about the good and the bad, their failures and successes, and their strengths and weaknesses. In this relationship, your teens want to share their good news with you, and they feel welcome to solicit your advice and prayers when they make mistakes.

The openness that friend status provides between parent and teen yields two major benefits for the safety and healthy development of the child. To the parent, it provides clarity for effective guidance. How can you know how to help if you don't know what the real issues are?

And to the teen, friend status provides accountability. After all, we'd hope the parent can do a better job of this than another teenager! When your teens are able to be honest with you on a more intimate level, and seek your counsel, they will likely behave more responsibly.

Some parents think, "My parents didn't try to be my friend, and I turned out good! So, why stray from the traditional parenting model that established respect and seemed to work, for the most part?"

Regardless of whether you want to hear it or not, times have changed. Society has changed. Technology has changed the way our world connects and the way our teens communicate. No, morals and values should not change; but, yes, approach MUST change if this generation will be reached effectively.

Think about it: You could've prepared an amazing care package for your hungry college student, containing all his favorite foods and sweet treats. But, what if you enclosed it in a garbage bag, and he threw it away because he couldn't recognize its value? Did your precious package benefit him if he never received it?

Likewise, you can have a great message, but the way you deliver that message determines whether or not it will be well-received. Our father teaches that **attitude determines approach, and approach determines success or failure**. Even in the midst of your emotions, remember that approach matters.

Have you ever been in an argument with someone, and they said, "Well, it's true!" in response to your furious reaction? Then, you thought, "Well, it wasn't *what* you said, but it was *how* you said it." **Understand that the wrong approach wraps the truth with offense, which hinders receptivity.**

On the other hand, if you learn to tactfully communicate with your teens, they are more prone to receive your wisdom and guidance.

Now let's talk about the accountability that friend status provides. There are certain things that we would not do with our boyfriends when we were teenagers because we thought of the questions our mom would ask when we got home. And lying was not an option!

She did not interrogate us, but she simply asked as a friend would about the details of our night: "Did he kiss you?" "Did he touch your bottom?" "Where did you go?" "Who was there?" "Did you have fun?" "Did he touch your breasts?"

During that time, there were physical things we were tempted to do and even desired to do that we did not do because of her.

She had already informed us about what we would encounter when dating, and she had asked us, "What will you do if he tries to…?" We knew from our detailed conversations (which she initiated) what she deemed acceptable and what wasn't.

We had developed such a loving, transparent relationship with our mom, and we were raised with such high moral standards that we knew we wouldn't lie when she asked all these questions. Therefore, there were certain things we would not do in order to avoid being embarrassed to tell Mom!

We will discuss later in this chapter how specifically she cultivated such

● ● ●

Understand that the wrong approach wraps the truth with offense, which hinders receptivity.

● ● ●

73

transparency in our relationship that invited the openness necessary for effective accountability.

Also, when you have an open relationship with your teens, you can help keep them accountable for the life goals they share with you in your intimate conversations.

When parents serve as this kind of unofficial accountability partner, they can have greater influence over their teens' mindsets and, therefore, decisions. And their teens will be more mindful not to disappoint them.

This level of influence actually sounds a lot like that effect your teen's friends consciously or subconsciously have on him/her called *peer pressure*. Used positively, it is a very powerful tool.

Before moving on, we do want to give a disclaimer for this topic. **Single parents must be very careful not to take the "friend" status too literally**. Sometimes, single parents take the attitude, "It's you and me against the world," and the parent makes the teen his/her best friend and even confidant.

This is not a position of security for the child. Your teen always needs to know you are the capable leader and decision-maker in the home who can handle the pressure that comes along with that leadership. Please don't make your teen carry that burden with you because they can't trust you enough to handle it on your own.

When both mom and dad are present, if one leans a little too far on the friendly side, the other parent can still provide security and command respect in the home. Single parents don't have that luxury.

● ● ●

Single parents must be very careful not to take the "friend" status too literally.

● ● ●

For single and two-parent households, the balance of so-called "friend" and "parent" status is delicate and highly important. Please remember that friend status does not mean your teen is equal to you in position and authority, but it is a symbolic term to represent the opportunity for the teen to be open and accountable to his/her parent.

Although you are always the parent by fact, the parent status (as we will refer to it) gives you the respect that is necessary for your teens to receive from you as a trusted authority figure and mentor, one whose words hold more weight than those of others.

The Danger of Extremes

There are always consequences for being too strict or too lenient as a parent. We'll first elaborate on the former.

Many strict parents have pure intentions. They are seeking to protect their teens using tight reins for control. What they might not realize is that their efforts can be counterproductive.

Teens often do what you forbid, just without your knowledge of it. When we were adolescents, we chatted with a teen girl and discovered that she wasn't allowed to date. She had a long history of ex-boyfriends and had a current boyfriend as well, despite her household's rule. We asked her if her parents knew, and she told us, "Of course not!"

This meant that her parents were not able to help guide her dating choices. She relied on her own judgment and that of her friends, which misled her every time.

Some would argue that, even if she did introduce them and they disapproved, the same rebellion would cause her to continue to date him despite their warning. While this could be true, your teens are more likely to care about your opinion if you have a healthy parent-teen relationship. Therefore, whether the change is made immediately or over time, your words will make a difference and will eventually provoke results.

We've personally experienced this "change over time" in our teenage dating relationships. When our parents made known their opinions of our boyfriends, we hated it! Our thoughts— "Here we go again… You don't like this one either? Who IS good enough then?!" But without fail, their words repeated in our heads and subconsciously highlighted our boyfriends' flaws. We knew it was only a matter of time before we had to break up with him, and we always did.

Imagine how differently these relationships would have gone if our parents were so strict that we didn't feel comfortable sharing with them. Their input on those boyfriends would have been nonexistent if the boyfriends were a secret.

Now, let's take a look at another pitfall of being too strict. A common example of the product of a strict parent is the student who waits for the day he is away from his parent's watchful eye. He then runs wild like a dog finally free from his leash, charging out the front door! These liberated prisoners begin to do everything they were never allowed to do: have premarital sex, drink alcohol, try drugs—you name it! This situation leaves the overprotective parent feeling bewildered, disappointed, and frustrated.

What about the teens who actually obey the strict parent? Well, some simply don't feel comfortable sharing their personal lives with their strict parents who obviously don't understand them (or so they think). They heed to the rules, they don't go wild, but they also don't come to their parents with their burdens, fears, or victories.

This scenario often breeds quiet resentment because of their perceived suffocation. It can also lead them to painfully suppress their emotions or to seek the guidance of foolish friends.

One student felt that his mother was overwhelmingly overprotective, so he joined the marines just to get away from her. Sadly, she probably never knew how strongly he despised her approach. You never want to operate in such a way that you drive your teens away from you, later regretting their bitter emotional departure.

Another student admitted that her mom was extremely difficult to talk to because every time she expressed herself, yelling, fussing, or nagging followed.

How can parents most effectively guide their teens if they have no clue how they think or what issues they're facing? Parents need to be able to offer relevant advice, which means they must know what's going on.

So yes, there are certainly negative consequences for being too strict. But, we would be remiss if we didn't also discuss the danger of being too lenient as a parent. Sometimes, teens feel like you don't care,

and they will act out merely to capture your attention.

One teenager told us that she disrespected her teacher and failed academically so that her parents would finally notice her.

Another student who we were mentoring received stern correction from us surprisingly well. She always apologized the same day or the following day for her actions, and she quickly implemented the changes that we recommended.

She expressed that she felt like we cared because we corrected her, and she wasn't accustomed to that. She presented a clear example of the verity that **teens equate a lack of adequate correction with a lack of concern.**

One guy that we interviewed even admitted that his parents could've been stricter. He said that he reached a point at which he had to start disciplining himself because he decided that he didn't want to become someone he wouldn't like. We discuss this more in the "Discipline that Works" chapter.

In other scenarios, teens enjoy the excessively lenient parent! They are having the time of their lives—or so they think. Their morality is degraded, and they are irresponsible. They might not understand the detriment immediately, but they certainly will suffer the consequences later in life.

We observed the detriment of parenting that was too liberal through a close friend when we were 14 years old. She was so sweet and well-behaved, and we had a lot in common with her. Her grades were commendable, and she was morally strong and conservative.

A year or two later, she left her biological father and her stepmother because she greatly missed her mother and wanted to live with her again. She described her mother as much more liberal than she was, but she loved and admired her. Her mom was a lot of fun, and was even open to taking her 13-year-old daughter to the parlor to get a tattoo with her!

When we were in college, we connected with her once again to discover that the conservative, reserved, sweet friend that we knew (who vowed to remain a virgin until marriage) had a baby out of wedlock, had extra piercings and tattoos (in contrast to her previous conservative nature), and was no longer participating in or even attending church.

From these examples and many more, we conclude that both parents who are too lenient and those who are too strict can end up raising rebellious, irresponsible, and resentful adults.

How Strict is Too Strict?

The Danger of Forbidding

"If they would give me the chance to prove myself, the chance to trust me, I would show them that I can do the right thing." —Anonymous Student

The statement above was expressed by a college student who said her parents were so strict that they forbid her and her siblings from virtually all fun! They set so many parameters for her that she felt trapped. Social events, sleepovers, ministry events— if it wasn't related to education, there wasn't room for it.

This student explained that her parents' habit of forbidding opened the door in her life to sneaking and lying. She felt like they completely stole her freedom to choose, so she took her own liberties behind their backs.

Some of the healthiest families contrast the typical parents who throw their weight around and always use the iron fist approach to rule their household. It's always, "I forbid you to…!"

While forbidding is sometimes necessary for certain personality types and maturity levels, it is not the only way. And it's definitely not the best way.

You might be surprised to find that some of the most well-behaved, responsible, and moral teens were not forbidden to do the things they chose not to do. They were given the opportunity to choose for themselves, and they made respectable decisions.

They observed the proper example modeled by their parents, maintained high respect for and open communication with their parents, and received productive counsel for moral and responsible living. When parents have captured the affection, trust, and respect of their teens, they hold a great deal of influence over their conscious decisions.

Helping teens understand *why* to do or not to do certain things versus just saying, "Because I said so," guides them to make the decision many parents would otherwise command.

Think about it: if the parent commands the teen to do something, which clearly is against the kid's will, it is evident that the child does not understand why he is making that decision.

Without knowing the "why" behind the "what," the teen often becomes resentful towards the parent. Depending upon the person, that lack of understanding can lead to rebellion.

The goal of parental guidance is not to create resentment and distance in the parent-teen relationship, but to foster growth and to provide protection. Therefore, **it's most effective to equip your teens to make the right choices, versus forcing them to ignorantly obey**. (You will read more about this in the ninth chapter, "Raising Great Decision-Makers.")

Again, we are not saying that occasional forbidding and commanding isn't necessary for your teen's safety, because sometimes it is. However, other methods that focus more on teaching are better when applicable.

Teach them values that will govern many of their decisions, and then guide them along the way, aiding their understanding of how to apply wisdom to their everyday life.

Dr. Tommy Barnett is a pastor of a megachurch and the founder (along with his son, Matthew Barnett) of the Dream Center, an astoundingly compassionate and effective charitable organization. In his book, *The Power of the Half Hour*, he discusses an excellent example of this guidance method that we're proposing.

● ● ●

It's most effective to equip your teens to make the right choices, versus forcing them to ignorantly obey.

● ● ●

Instead of forbidding his children to listen to certain kinds of music, Dr. Barnett asked them thought-provoking questions. This caused them to evaluate their desire to listen to a particular type of music.

He taught them about the power of music and its influence over their thoughts. He discussed the conflict of values between their instilled beliefs and the popular music, as well as the impact of that exposure on who they'd become.

After sharing his advice, he left his teens with the opportunity to choose. Keep in mind that he had an open relationship with his kids, and they admired their father a great deal.

With this kind of freedom, were his children wild and undisciplined? No. Even though the other kids were listening to the music that was most popular, his teens chose to listen to music that would influence them according to their belief system.

They didn't feel oppressed and controlled, but rather, cared for and educated. Not only did they make the right choice in this instance, but also more holistically. Through this "non-forbidding" method, they grew closer to their parents, and they became more responsible decision-makers.

They all embraced the values instilled, not forced, in them by their parents, and they eventually chose paths of full-time ministry like their parents did (demonstrating their admiration!).

Likewise, our parents did not practice a lot of forbidding. They would calmly explain certain matters, share convicting wisdom, set expectations, and charge us to make the right choices.

We were very clear about what they wanted us to do, such as who they thought we should be friends with and who they didn't, but they had other ways of limiting our access to those people without explicitly forbidding us. We share more about those tactics in the "Purposeful Protection" chapter.

Honestly, they led our home as such inspirational examples that they didn't even have to talk to us about some things: we naturally wanted to be like them, which often steered us in the right direction.

As we said, our parents normally did not forbid us from doing certain things, but rather taught us what we *should* do. There are, however, a few instances where they did forbid us, and we will tell you how those turned out…

When we were elementary school age, our mom entered the room as we were watching a Halloween episode of *Rugrats* on

Nickelodeon. She actually walked in during the introductory music, which was creepy-sounding, as is typical for Halloween themes. Anyway, she proceeded to say something like the following: "What is this?! This sounds scary! Turn this off and do not ever watch this show again!"

We were absolutely horrified! This was one of our favorite shows, and it was only an innocent cartoon! We thought her command was unwarranted, unnecessary, and unfair. We refused to be suppressed by such tyranny (or so we thought ☺)!

Therefore, in the future, we still watched *Rugrats*: she just didn't know about it. We arranged the channels in such a way that we simply had to press the flashback button when we heard her coming. That way, she only saw us watching the so-called "acceptable" shows.

She also told us that we couldn't watch *Scooby Doo* because of all the scary components, causing nightmares, creating paranoia, and instilling fear. So, we watched it at our grandparents' house.

She said we couldn't watch *Dawson's Creek* because it was more of an adult's program AND it aired weekly at our 8:00 p.m. bedtime. We watched it anyway, in her room, sitting on her bed while she was at choir rehearsal on Wednesday nights.

Furthermore, she said we couldn't watch *How Stella Got Her Groove Back*, and we enjoyed admiring Taye Diggs in this engaging film anyway. Haha! This was yet another forbidden pleasure that we enjoyed in her room with popcorn until we heard our outdoor dog barking. He was our alarm meaning, "Mom and Dad are home!" And we all took off running! The rule was that the last sibling out the door turns off the TV and the lights.

The moral of the story is that forbidding often doesn't work, even with the most darling, well-mannered children! ☺

Now let's clarify that young kids haven't developed the judgment necessary to be equipped to make their own decisions. Therefore, it is often necessary for them to be forbidden, even if they don't understand.

But by the time they are mature enough or at some point in

their teenage years, they should be treated as young adults, learning to make good decisions. This is why a 4-year-old isn't insulted when you tell him how to eat or dress, but when you try that with your 16-year-old, it's a major problem.

Adolescents should be prepared to make responsible decisions, and that means their decisions shouldn't all be made for them. Of course, there are exceptions to every rule, so use wisdom. But, the older that people become, the more they desire independence, which is natural because they do need the room to mature.

One of our sisters was probably a freshman in college when Dad forbade her to date a certain boy that was pursuing her. Next thing you know, they were in love! She couldn't seem to let him go until Dad later wrote her a heartfelt letter helping her to understand his perspective and explaining the importance of moving on. Yes, teens will sometimes just be hard-headed, but a better approach can help.

In addition, several of the teens that we grew up around were forbidden to date until they were 16 years old. Everyone BUT their parents knew who their sweethearts were. Consequently, the parents were not able to meet the significant other or give feedback about their dating choices.

Our parents did not give us a dating age requirement, but rather discussed with us the importance of our maturity level, dating the right kind of person, and establishing wholesome boundaries.

Our parents met each person we ever had interest in. And whether we wanted to admit it or not, their approval made a huge difference in the longevity, or lack thereof, of our relationships.

If they disapproved, even if it took a while for us to break up with the person, we could no longer feel as comfortable in that relationship. We had the kind of relationship with our parents in which we truly valued their opinion.

Parents that forbid are normally left out of the loop of their teens' lives. The teen feels deprived of his right to choose and feels like the parent doesn't understand his point of view.

The alternative is modeling the proper example, teaching the desired values, explaining the "why" behind the "what," and charging your teen to make the right choices.

When parents forbid, teens can become angry *just because*. Even if they don't think you're crazy for your desire to establish that rule, the lack of trust and freedom that forbidding demonstrates is what is most upsetting. In addition, it's just plain annoying to your kids. Haha! You want to inspire your teens through your leadership, not annoy or provoke them. There are certainly more effective ways to develop your teens than forbidding them.

The Danger of Overreacting

The radically concerned mother of a teenage young lady pleaded with us to help her wild daughter. When we conducted the counseling session with the teen girl, who was described as highly rebellious and sneaky, we discovered something that probably would have shocked her mother.

She seemed sweet and very aware of her need to change. In fact, she had the desire to change. She felt that the root of her misbehavior was her relationship with her mother. She was misbehaving because she was intentionally rebelling against what she perceived as oppression from her mom.

The girl believed that her mother overreacted about everything, whether big or small. She felt she could not be honest with her mom because it would initiate fierce yelling. So, instead, she lied.

Also, she told us that her mom made a lot of assumptions about her and held tight reins on her. She described each of their conversations as arguments because her mother would start yelling.

We asked her, "What do you think you can do to repair your relationship with your mom?" She replied, "I could be honest despite her reaction and then keep my mouth shut throughout the yelling session."

She didn't feel welcome to share her struggles with her mom. Therefore, instead of seeking her mother for advice for her schoolwork and relationships, she sought her friends, who were major distractions.

She described her most significant hindrance to growth as her broken relationship with

One of the single most important keys to maintaining open communication with your teens is NOT overreacting.

her mom, which consisted of little to no communication. During the chats she did have with her mother, she infused the conversation with lies to avoid the notorious yelling.

A few months later, her mother contacted us, again panicking, but this time because her frustrated daughter had run away from home.

One of the single most important keys to maintaining open communication with your teens is NOT overreacting. It is a mistake that probably most parents around the world make. It is a natural reaction that is born of intense anger, frustration, shock, or disappointment due to alarming information.

Honestly, it's easy to overreact to issues in areas of your passion, which should include your teens.

Therefore, it takes self-discipline to control your responses so you that you don't overreact. The truth is, you might see your dramatic response as proof that you care; meanwhile, your teens see your overreacting as nothing beautiful like passion, but rather something dreaded, offensive, and annoying.

You should make it a habit to always respond instead of react. We define a reaction in this context as an emotional impulse that is comprised of whatever the person *feels* like doing or saying in the moment. Often, reactions are accompanied by yelling, cursing, and harsh statements if the news is disappointing.

Even if what you are saying is true, be careful to communicate respectfully, lovingly, and in a way that does not insult the character of your teen.

Actions should be addressed in a way that corrects, yet makes your child feel capable of doing better. This happens through encouragement. Your teen should never leave a discussion with you feeling worthless.

In contrast to reactions, we can think of responses as products of thought, not emotion. We should always aim to respond after considering the most appropriate and beneficial way of communicating our thoughts.

And in order to respond most appropriately, parents must first seek to understand their teen's perspective.

Some parents want to know how to go from "ancient" to "relevant" in their teen's eyes—in other words, how to relate better. It is quite simple. You don't have to pose as some cool kid that you're not or all of a sudden "speak their language."

What you do need to do to relate to them is seek to understand their world, their perspective, their interests, and their problems. This way, you can more effectively communicate with them.

As we'll discuss more later, when you respond to them, repeat back to them what they communicated to you (accurately, not a distorted interpretation of it) in order to let them know you understand where they are coming from. Then, proceed with your thoughts about the subject matter in a calm, concerned tone.

> *Okay, so you are saying that you didn't mean to disrespect your teacher, but when he touched you, you felt threatened and raised your fist in defense? Is that what you're saying? Okay, I definitely understand how you could feel that way, and I appreciate your honesty so that I didn't have to hear it from the school. That takes integrity. Thank you. Now in the future, even though you may feel threatened, I would advise you to...*

When you carefully respond instead of impulsively react, you can understand more clearly what your teen is thinking and feeling. You can keep the doors of honest communication open to you, and you can offer wise counsel. No matter how you feel, remember not to scare off your teens!

We can very clearly remember a humiliating situation in which we made a bad decision and our mother found out. Even still, she proved that she could handle the truth. She responded wisely, in a way we'll always remember...

When we were in high school, we failed to come directly home one night after the evening service at church. We weren't driving ourselves, but we were in the car with our boyfriends. Sooo... it was a little late, and we decided to make a stop to make out somewhere.

Just in case this terminology is new to you, "to make out" means "to engage in prolonged kissing." Haha! We wanted a private place that wasn't too much of a detour along the way home, so one of us thought it was a good idea to stop at the playground right outside of our neighborhood.

One of the couples stayed in the car to kiss, and the other couple went to the swings. Since the park was not a 24-hour operation, there were no lights on the playground—how perfect for kissing!

To clarify, we had never before made a kissing detour to the playground at night. We had told our parents that we were going to eat at Waffle House up the street on the way home from the evening service. Technically, we did not lie because we did quickly eat there and then decided our time would be better spent kissing.

For some reason, maybe the voice of the Lord, our mom drove by Waffle House 20-30 minutes after we left. Then, she immediately drove to the playground!

As we said, one couple was kissing in the car, so they felt like deer in headlights when her car's lights pierced through the back windshield of the car. They were shocked, horrified, and humiliated!

Although the guy pretended to be asleep when she came around to the passenger's seat that we were sharing, Mom was no fool. She was hurt, disappointed, and angry, yet calm.

She asked us where the other sister and her boyfriend were, since she knew they were there with us. After all, we were in her boyfriend's car.

When we pointed to the dark playground, she appeared so concerned and upset that we were frightened. She called their names, and they took the walk of shame out of the shadows to greet Dr. Nina Bronner.

She explained the danger of being outside in complete darkness, late at night, and without anyone knowing where we were. She also expressed her disappointment that we omitted to tell her about our second destination.

Because she knew us and we knew her, she didn't have to say much—which she didn't—and she didn't have to yell—which she didn't—in order for us to understand the error of our actions. We felt immediate remorse for disappointing her so greatly and felt so humiliated that we were positive we would never do that again.

Even though we were afraid because we were caught in such a compromising situation, it was not her response that provoked our fear. She did not overreact at all, nor did she tell anyone else—ever.

There was clear communication concerning what was wrong, why it was wrong, and how she perceived our actions. She could tell by our shameful demeanor that we understood and that we felt the sting of our actions. Therefore, she did not aim to further humiliate us by telling the rest of the family what we did.

She did just what was necessary, and that demonstrated to us mercy, love, and truth in a powerful way that we will never forget.

As far as we can remember, our parents have always been wonderful examples of this mercy. When we were in elementary school, I (Kristie) got really angry about something and stormed out of my parents' room into the upstairs hallway of our home. Next thing you know, I kicked one of the white, wooden poles that held up the balcony rail.

To my shock, it snapped in half! I, then, ran to my room in tears of anger that turned into tears of terror, waiting for the punishment and yelling with my name on it.

To my surprise, my parents did not yell at me. Instead, they responded calmly and tactfully. They could tell that I was already frightened and remorseful, so they chose to say only what was necessary. Because they didn't overreact, I reflected on why I was wrong, repented, and never broke anything out of frustration again.

This, along with many other instances, taught us at an early age that we did not have to hide from our parents. They would not overreact, but rather correct us in love.

They would not kill us over making a mistake because they did not hold us to a standard of perfection. They never made us feel like we could never be good enough or that we would not be accepted UNLESS... Even when we broke dishes, although we weren't allowed to use glass until we got a little older, we always knew that we were more important than our mistakes and more valuable than anything we could ever break.

Through the consistency of our parents' responses and teachings, we came to trust their character. We knew their goal was to protect and develop us, not to hurt or humiliate us.

Yes, there were consequences for our actions: we got spankings and lectures and lost privileges. But, we knew they wouldn't scream or kick us out of the house if they found out something that disappointed them. We learned that we didn't have to withhold information or tell "cover up" lies because we could trust them. **Because they didn't overreact to the truth, we knew we were safe to share it with them.**

The Keys to Openness

"I'm the parent, so I just tell my child what it's gonna be—end of story. What more is there to talk about? When I was that age, my parents were the law, my opinions didn't matter, and I turned out fine."—Stubborn, Old-Fashioned Parent

While it may be true that the "iron fist" approach proved effective in the past, and some great people were raised that way, parenting now has to look different from parenting "back then." Why? Because the culture now is different than it once was.

Parents have to learn how to reach teens in *their* cultural context, not one of the past.

For example, the prevalence of social media has introduced a new era of transparency. People are sharing pictures, videos, and thoughts from their everyday life on Facebook, Twitter, Vine, Instagram, Snapchat, and more! Privacy is losing value, and the world seems smaller by the day.

Now that this openness has become the new norm, it's even more important for teens to feel comfortable sharing their lives with their parents. They apparently have the need to share if they are exposing their thoughts, problems, and emotions to the rest of the world already!

Surely enough, if they aren't sharing everything with you, they're sharing it with someone, and that someone might not be a wise choice. They could even be disclosing *too* much and need *you* to reel them back in.

Additionally, kids are being exposed to sex, drugs, and other obscenities at younger ages than they once were. Therefore, whereas certain topics discussed between parent and child used to be taboo, openness and real conversations with your teens are becoming more and more necessary.

Communication Barriers

Mom: "You did WHAT?! How could you have been so stupid?! I'm shocked at your behavior, and I can't believe you would even dream of doing something so foolish! You could not have been thinking at all. I can't even process this right now."

Teen: "But, Mom..."

Mom: "Ah, ah! I don't want to hear it. You're gonna listen to ME right now. The only one in this room with some good sense... I'm taking away your

● ● ●

If you want transparency in your parent-teen relationship, listen without overreacting.

● ● ●

phone, your iPad, your TV, your driving privileges, and all of your social time for the next two months. Don't even think about saying anything else to me about it."

When we ask students why they don't feel comfortable sharing with their parents, the most common response is "They always overreact!" Remember that, as we previously discussed in "The Danger of Overreacting" subsection of the second section ("How Strict is Too Strict?") of "Friend or Parent," **overreacting is one of the fastest ways to close the door of communication**.

Furthermore, not only do teens complain that parents overreact, but they also complain that parents don't listen. "They never listen to me. When I try to express myself, they cut me off and keep yelling. What's the point?"

If you want transparency in your parent-teen relationship, listen without overreacting.

Good friends make each other feel loved, accepted, and welcome to share. A parent probably wouldn't be someone you would share your secrets with if you felt like he/she would, as American youth like to say, "jump down your throat" over every little thing. Yes, correction is necessary, but so are tact and patience.

When you cultivate openness in your relationship with your teens, as we discuss in the "The Benefit of Both" subsection of the second section of "Friend or Parent" entitled "How Strict is Too Strict," you have the access to serve as an unofficial accountability partner for them. This accountability is some of the best protection you can give them! Therefore, let's discuss how to acquire this intimacy.

Building Trust

Just as developing friendships involves gaining trust, you must gain your teen's trust. You do this by being authentic, trustworthy, and transparent.

If you want them to be open with you as a friend, be open with them yourself. Let them see who you are. Don't be afraid to show them your personality. They don't have to see only your strict side in order to respect you. Let them see your silly side and how much fun you really can be! Let them understand that you are a multifaceted human being.

● ● ●

As we've often heard our father say, "You teach what you know, but you reproduce who you are."

● ● ●

Be honest with them. For some reason, parents tell their kids not to lie, but they justify telling lies to their kids! It starts off with the "friendly" lies, like "Santa Claus is coming to eat these cookies," and "The tooth fairy will exchange money for your loose tooth."

Then, "Your father (who just abandoned the family) is just on vacation. He'll be back soon." Next thing you know… "Say good morning to your Uncle Tommy" (who isn't really your uncle). Next week… "Meet your Uncle Michael. I was just showing him the family album in my bedroom." Some kids are even 18 years old exclaiming, "What do you mean you're not my biological father?!"

As we've often heard our father say, **"You teach what you know, but you reproduce who you are." You cannot lie to your teens and expect honesty in return.** Although you should be tactful in your communication with your kids at young and old ages, you should always make honesty your policy. Lying to your teens models poor character for them and damages the relationship as soon as they discover the truth.

Beyond being honest with your teens, you can show yourself to be trustworthy by upholding standards of confidentiality. You should never tell their secrets (unless it is an emergency), make fun of them in humiliating ways (even if you think it's cute or funny), or repeat anything they've told you in confidence (even when you're upset).

As we mention in the "Powerful Language" chapter, we've had numerous parents approach us at church with their teenager under their arm, talking about their teen in his/her presence as if the kid had no pride or feelings!

They would say something like this:

> *Hi! I want you to meet my son, Martin. He is sixteen, he goes to Pebblebrook High School, and he is going down a wrong path. He is failing in school, distracted by all the girls, and I have to practically drag him to church with me! He's quite stubborn and has a bit of a temper. I wanted him to meet you so that maybe he can get inspired to live right and make better grades. Tell him about the youth programs here that you ladies offer.*

The mom is grinning eagerly like what she just said was somehow okay, and the teen is trying his best not to roll his eyes or shrink away in humiliation. It's still amazing how those kids managed to keep their composure under that level of anger and embarrassment! Sadly, it seems to happen so often that they are numb to it.

There is no excuse for telling a stranger all of your teen's personal business (and in front of them!) unless you are in a counseling session.

Our parents never divulged our secrets or betrayed our trust, but we could understand on a small scale the embarrassment parents can cause unknowingly…

For some absurd reason, when we were about twelve years

old, our mom thought it was cute to tell our entire slumber party the most embarrassing details possible!!! Everyone was laughing as she chatted with them, and then she began to allude to something that provoked us to think, "Oh, surely, she wouldn't bring that up..." Next thing you know, she did!

She told them about a mole on one of our bottoms, and she specified *who*! The exposed twin was absolutely horrified. This twin immediately turned red and left the room. She was too embarrassed to even enjoy the rest of the sleepover. That wasn't cool.

You might wonder, just like we did, what possessed Mom to think that was acceptable to share? To our surprise, though, Mom was completely unaware of the humiliation that she caused.

She actually had a tendency to share embarrassing things about her kids and even her husband. Nevertheless, when she learned how certain kinds of comments made us feel, she restrained herself on those topics. As a result of her adjustment, we still let her talk to our friends. Haha! 😊

Even though that instance didn't feel like a light matter at the time, it was relatively trivial compared to much weightier matters...

A late night counseling session I (Kristie) had with a teenager broke my heart. She was in tears about a romantic relationship that had just ended. She admitted that, even if she and her ex-boyfriend did get back together, their relationship wouldn't be healthy because she didn't trust him.

To myself, I thought, "Well, it sounds to me like you need to stay away from that cheater anyway!" Then, she confessed that the fault was hers. It wasn't just him that she couldn't trust. She couldn't trust anyone.

When I asked her about the root of her broken trust, she cried even harder as she explained that everyone close to her, including her own parents, had exposed every secret that she had told them in confidence. She also told me that both of her parents had lied to her. She was heartbroken, bitter, and consequently, defensive.

Parents should never be among the number that betrays the trust of their teens.

Most common cases of this betrayal occur when parents bring up one of their teen's past mistakes in front of another family member or friend.

> *Parents should never be among the number that betrays the trust of their teens.*

While in arguments with their teen, some parents say inappropriate things like, "See, that's why you shouldn't have smoked weed that time! I think it damaged some of your brain cells! Stop being so hard-headed, and listen!"

Whether in front of others or in private, never bring up your teen's past mistakes out of anger. One student expressed the following sentiments on this subject:

> *I felt like they didn't understand because they were perfect and I already messed up. Instead of condemning me for my mistakes and not letting me live it down, they should have disciplined me and forgiven me and stopped bringing it back up. I felt like they would hold onto stuff, even if it's just one thing. I felt like, "What's the point of trying to do right when they're just going to hold onto that one thing that I did wrong?" It should have been more of a teaching spirit than a disciplinarian one. I wish my parents would have been more open and less judgmental. I chose not to communicate with them because I knew how they would react.*

The process of changing can be very discouraging when people close to you, like your parents, constantly hold your mistakes against you. Additionally, no one wants to share their problems and regrets with someone they cannot trust to keep quiet and to remain non-judgmental.

Remember that love doesn't keep a record of wrongs, and anger doesn't warrant regurgitation of past issues. Negativity achieves nothing positive. It merely destroys trust and hinders growth.

One thing our parents never did was share our mistakes, issues, or secrets with anyone else, including other family members. They did, however, maintain boundaries and tell us the truth about our situation. They told us that we could trust them, and they proved it.

This allowed us the freedom to remove restraint when sharing our lives with them.

The Power of Transparency

"We didn't keep things hidden from the kids, separating adult issues from what we thought was youth appropriate. I believe that is one reason why our children never got bitter toward us; they knew we were honest with them and that we would address the things that were on their minds." —Dr. Tommy Barnett (*The Power of the Half Hour*)

Probably the most important key to opening the door of communication is transparency. Just like the concept, "You have to give respect in order to get respect," **you must be transparent to encourage transparency**.

When we conduct panel discussions at our youth conferences and youth services, we observe an abundance of transparency in our audience after the panel shares. Youth wait in long lines to tell their life stories, pain, violations, and darkest secrets.

Our panelists always model the highest levels of transparency by sharing the so-called "skeletons in their closets" in front of hundreds of people. They are down-to-earth, free to

● ● ●

Remember that love doesn't keep a record of wrongs, and anger doesn't warrant regurgitation of past issues.

● ● ●

be themselves even in the spotlight, and relatable. It is no surprise that the youth respond by rushing to talk to them as soon as they exit the stage!

In addition, when our mother talked to us about our personal business, she would always share a piece of her own. She made a habit of sharing a story from her past, whether dating relationships or emotional states.

She used to tell us details of her past relationships, describing the person, the nature of the relationship, and the mistakes she made. She was even transparent about her current life, her weaknesses, failures, strengths, and successes. Whatever the case, she opened up first.

She would say, "I told you my business: now, tell me yours." She said this, not as manipulation or as a demand, but as encouragement from a friend.

You might wonder how we developed healthy respect for our mother with this kind of relationship. The truth is that we had to learn the balance between openness and reverence. When you have this kind of transparency in your parent-teen relationship, your teen's self-expression can be so passionate that it comes off disrespectful sometimes.

As teenage girls, we occasionally expressed ourselves with so much emotion that it came across harshly. Our mother would say, "Now, I know you don't mean to be disrespectful, but..." She chose to tactfully correct us in these scenarios while maintaining open communication.

It's your choice: either you want 100% reverence without honesty, or you want transparency at the cost of utmost reverence. **You can have both parent and friend status, but a PERFECT balance is a fairy tale.**

The primary reason we maintained tremendous respect for our mother is that she is an extraordinarily respectable person. It was okay for us to know her completely because she had nothing she needed to hide. She was the same person at church and at home. We could see that there wasn't a hypocritical bone in her body.

Trust us: your teens notice your weaknesses anyway. You might as well be honest when you think it could help them. It liberates them to be open with you.

We could also respect the profound wisdom that we received from her as we enjoyed those in-depth chats. She taught us invaluable lessons, and she kept us from making some very bad choices. Because she knew what we were planning, she was able to explain to us why we should choose otherwise.

She made herself approachable. She would even apologize for her mistakes as a parent. This taught us the value of humility. We learned that you are never too important or too perfect to apologize for your shortcomings.

We also learned lasting lessons from the stories she told us about her past mistakes. We remembered those mental pictures she painted for us far better than bare principles taught without relatable examples.

She created an environment of non-judgment, love, and learning. It made us feel comfortable to talk to her, and we knew that she would not overreact. In this intimate relationship, we did not abuse this non-judgmental and loving culture because we valued her opinion and respected her. We did not want to disappoint her.

She would also ask us a lot of questions about our friendships, dating relationships, life at school, and family life. Believe it or not, we actually answered most of her questions.

Not only did we answer her questions, but also, we offered her extra details of our personal lives because we enjoyed talking to her. We loved sharing with her and hearing her feedback.

One day, as our mom was waking up from a nap, we ran into her room and jumped on her bed to share our exciting news. "Mom! We're gonna have our first kiss next Saturday at Six Flags!" We were fourteen years old.

She paused for a second, took a breath, and calmly continued to listen. We proceeded to tell her all of the details, including who would sit on the front row of the Monster's Plantation boat (Six Flags ride) and who on the second. Haha!

One of us had a boyfriend, and one of us was in the "get-to-know-you" stage with someone who shouldn't have even been a candidate!

Our parents had discussed not having sex before marriage ever since before we knew what sex was, and we had already vowed to remain virgins until we were married.

However, they had forgotten to talk to us about kissing. Therefore, under the influence of our society, we felt that we were behind everyone else. After all, everyone else had already had their first kiss! (or so we thought...)

Mom was quite alarmed. Nevertheless, she did not overreact, yell, or forbid us to kiss. Instead, she talked to us very calmly about what she called "awakening the sleeping giant (your hormones)," and she advised us against doing so. She begged us to wait until we were sixteen years old, and we reluctantly consented.

After this unforgettable dialogue in her bedroom, we conversed with each other about how much we regretted telling Mom our plans. She made a lot of sense, so we knew we wouldn't feel comfortable continuing as planned. And of course, our "kissing buddies" weren't happy either. Haha!

Still, not only did Mom get her way because we honored her request, but also she got even more than what she asked for because we actually waited until we were seventeen years old to kiss.

In addition, to this day, we sometimes converse about how glad we are that we didn't kiss those boys that Saturday!

The fact that she fostered so much openness in our relationship that we felt comfortable talking to her about most situations of our lives allowed her to have greater influence on our mindsets than most other parents do.

Just to clarify, this chapter discusses Mom's role in our openness instead of Dad's because we are girls! It is ideal for mothers to have these uncomfortable chats with their daughters and fathers with their sons, when possible.

Of course, in single-parent households, you have to work with what you have. But in our home, Dad talked to us personally about the value of virginity, took us to buy our purity rings, treated us to a nice dinner date to sign a sexual purity covenant, and laid a firm foundation for us. He was (and still is!) a major influence in our lives, shaping our character and values, while our mom handled the day-to-day accountability questions with the dirty details.

Now, let's talk about some other teens' experiences with transparency in their homes.

One guy explained that his mom would be more relatable and easy to talk to if she didn't "paint herself so goody-goody, wholesome, and clean." He felt like she depicted herself as one that didn't make the mistakes that most make. It seemed to him that she didn't even try to relate to him and his siblings.

"She should've avoided being judgmental, and she should've made more effort to acknowledge people's differences, instead of judging others based upon her own life," he said. According to him, she did not convince him that she would love and accept her kids for who they are and how they are.

He described the primary reason that he didn't have transparency in his relationship with his parents as a "barrier" between their differing perspectives. He said that his parents were so involved in church that he was intimidated by them, thinking that they would judge him if he shared his problems with them.

Although his assumptions about their judging him might have been based only upon his feelings, his parents could've been more transparent with him.

Maybe if they were open with him about their past, their mistakes, and their weaknesses, he would've realized that he could relate to them, and therefore, felt comfortable to share more with them.

Believe it or not, revealing some of your past and current flaw s can earn more respect in the eyes of your teens, not less. If they see you as perfect, they will feel discouraged about trying to live up to the standard set by your life's example. You never want them to feel like they can't achieve greatness because it seems too far-fetched.

One girl felt like the relationship between her and her parents was hindered because her parents always seemed so perfect, and their perfection was simply far too unrealistic for her to attempt to live up to. Note her powerful words below:

> My parents never tried to pull themselves off that pedestal or tried to pull down that idea of perfection. They never tried to come down to earth. They didn't have any experiences and didn't know how to understand. Didn't relate well. They should have let me know that they don't expect perfection and that they love me and that they aren't perfect.

The truth is, her parents did have experiences to share and definitely had flaws: they just didn't let her see them.

Modeling vulnerability by opening up first is key. **No one wants to make himself vulnerable without proof that his thoughts are safe with you.** You must create an atmosphere of freedom and non-judgment by sharing your own imperfections before you inquire about others'.

When swallowing your pride to be transparent, remember the goal. If you do your part to keep the door of communication open, you can gain the access that normally only teens' peers are privileged to have.

Just imagine how much wiser your teens would be if they sought counsel from those who would give them wisdom instead of from those who tell them to do what is most popular at the moment.

● ● ●

No one wants to make himself vulnerable without proof that his thoughts are safe with you.

● ● ●

Erasing the ~~"Little White"~~ LIE

Many people think that lying teenagers are synonymous with speeding drivers: they know it's wrong, but somehow it seems unavoidable and fairly acceptable. Well, what if we told you that not all teenagers lie to their parents? We, nor our siblings (to our knowledge), made a habit of lying to our parents as we were growing up.

Our parents were so wise that they taught us from a young age that the truth is the only expected and acceptable option in our home. First of all, they modeled honesty, which we discuss in the "Building Trust" subsection of "The Keys to Openness" (the third section of the tenth chapter, "Friend or Parent.")

They were honest with us, with one another, and with others. They never instructed us to answer the phone and tell someone they're not home, no matter how dreaded the call. They made honesty their policy despite the cost.

Secondly, they attempted to instill this practice in us during conflict. For example, when we were elementary school age, if one of us broke a sculpture or wrote on the wall, they would gather all five kids and go down the line asking each child who did it. They prefaced the interrogation with the following: "If you tell us the truth, you will not be spanked; but, if you lie to us, then we will spank you."

We still lied. In one instance, I (Kirstie, the one who committed the "household crime") blamed it on my brother since he was the only one who never got the spankings he deserved! They believed it, and he was punished. I, the real culprit, got away free and satisfied!

Apparently, their honesty lesson didn't work that time. Nevertheless, this honesty ideology stuck with us for the future. We grew up with the resolve that, in spite of what trouble the truth could cause, there is no other way to live and communicate.

Lastly, when we were in middle school and high school, our parents would verbally acknowledge our freedom to be transparent with them. Our mom actually told us that she would never kick us out, regardless of what happened, even if we did the unthinkable. She expressed that she would always love us and that we could come to her about anything, under any circumstances.

Of the numerous teens and young adults that we have interviewed and the abundance of youth that we have encountered, the consistent feedback concerning why they lie to their parents is centered on their parents' responses. They fear their parents' reaction—the yelling, name-calling, punishments, threats, and disappointment.

There are always exceptions, but maybe if parents verbally gave teens the freedom to be transparent, modeled honesty, and refused to overreact, then more teens would admit the truth.

Although our parents maintained high standards, they always made us feel like they understood our humanity and our vulnerability to make mistakes. They never demanded perfection, but rather they encouraged responsible behavior in us by constantly reaffirming our identity.

Our parents' example of honesty, memorable lessons about truth, calm responses, and understanding of our imperfections empowered us to be honest with them. This freedom to make mistakes (which will be made anyway) and to be honest about them was instrumental to our openness throughout our adolescence and into our adulthood.

Active Listening & Respect

Active Listening

When asked how her parents could relate to her better, Katy said her parents could "actually listen when she tries to talk." She went on to express that when they ask her questions, they don't even let her finish responding before they interject.

Katy needed her parents to listen. She needed to be heard. And the lack in that area caused automatic strain on their relationship.

The truth is that everyone likes a good listener. **Any relationship built upon monologues versus dialogues will breed dysfunction.** The parent-teen relationship is no exception. This relationship must be built upon mutual respect and healthy communication, which both require listening.

People do not feel respected if it seems like they don't have a voice. If they're not allowed to express their opinion, they don't feel valued. Communication is then cheapened.

Because everyone has a basic need to be heard and understood, people naturally gravitate towards those who listen intently and respond thoughtfully.

People who extend themselves as exceptional listeners without judgment often serve as counselors unofficially, yet frequently. Regardless of who you are or what you value, people are drawn to you when you have great communication skills.

With this in mind, consider that you might not approve of whatever random kid is a great listener for your teen. And that person, whoever it may be, not only hears what's on your teen's mind, but also has permission to respond. This is a position of influence. That's why it's vital for you to communicate effectively with your teens. **Don't let the available take the position of the qualified!**

Keep in mind that communication is the basis of all relationships. If you always exalt your own opinion and don't take the time to listen to, much less, consider your teens' opinions, they will never feel close to you.

In every relationship, including the one between parents and their teens, there should be boundaries of respect. Your teens should respect you, and you should model respect by respecting them. This means that while you're talking, they do not.

● ● ●

Don't let the available take the position of the qualified!

● ● ●

They listen to you and refrain from rolling their eyes, putting their headphones in, or mentally tuning you out. They do not talk over you in attempts to interject with their defense or justification before you've finished.

The same is true in reverse. They talk; you listen. They should always be allowed to express themselves to you fully and uninterrupted, of course in a respectful tone and using respectful language. When they finish, you never overreact, as we previously discussed. You simply respond in love and truth.

If they do begin raising their voices or revealing too much anger in their tone while expressing themselves, let them finish, and model the proper response in dialogue.

Let them know *after* the discussion that you want them to express themselves, but that they should be careful of the tone and volume of their voice while doing so. Teach them to remain calm and respectful while communicating, even when they feel flustered. Tell them, and demonstrate it for them.

In contrast, if you interrupt them in the moment, they probably won't complete their thoughts and will become even more emotional, preceding a complete shut-down.

When people are emotional, they often aren't thinking very rationally. Therefore, they perceive your attempt to correct their tone as your intent to stifle their self-expression. Example: "You *said* you wanted me to express myself, but then when I did, you cut me off! Just forget it!"

Remember that, when people are emotional, they aren't as aware of their tone. They might sound angry or frustrated, but it might not be directed at you! Yes, it should be corrected, but approach and timing are everything.

If our mom cut us off every time our tone sounded somewhat inappropriate, we would not have been open with her. Usually if we sounded disrespectful, it was unintentional. Yes, we were angry sometimes, and it showed; but, we often felt remorseful and apologized to her later.

She always believed the best about us and demonstrated grace that seemed almost un-human (angelic, I guess!) at times. In some instances, when we sounded too agitated during our venting sessions, she would gently say something like, "I know you didn't mean to be disrespectful, but be careful of your tone. Okay, Sweetie Pie?"

Imagine if you encourage self-expression, and one day your teens are being honest with you about how you've hurt or offended them. Especially if it were an accumulation of instances being discussed… Their voice might start off calm, and later, when their emotions escalate, the tone might sound a little less objective.

It takes certain personality types or great maturity to master communication with complete emotional control, so have patience with your young ones. And teach them!

You should encourage them to talk to you about anything, and then actually listen when they do. We must emphasize that this "good listening" is free from all interjections and dramatic reactions.

We have heard numerous youth say, "Every time I *try* to talk to my mom/dad, then…"

- They never hear me out.
- They always overreact.
- They always cut me off.
- They only listen to themselves talk.
- They never care what I think.
- They always do everything their own way.

These common communication barriers can discourage your teens from discussing meaningful issues with you. **A clear-cut way to conceptualize how to be an effective listener is being to your teen the kind of listener you wish your spouse were to you!**

According to Peter Scazzero's *Emotionally Healthy Spirituality*, here are some tips for important conversations as you aim to listen intently and communicate effectively (pp. 187-188):

- **As the speaker...**
  - Talk about your own thoughts, your own feelings.
    - *[To clarify, this means that you should avoid accusations and instead focus on expressing how the situation made you feel. Seek to connect with the heart of your listener instead of attacking your listener. A great way to accomplish this is to make yourself vulnerable by statements such as "That made me feel _____," instead of "YOU did _____."]*
  - Be brief. Use short sentences or phrases.
  - Correct the other person if you believe he or she has missed something.
  - Continue speaking until you feel you've been understood.
  - When you don't have anything else to say, say, "That's all for now."
- **As the listener...**
  - Put your own agenda on hold. Be quiet and still.
  - Allow the other person to speak until he or she completes a thought.
  - Reflect accurately the other person's words back to him or her. You have two

options: paraphrase in a way the other person agrees is accurate or use his or her own words. (e.g. "Okay, so you are saying that it makes you feel belittled when I make comparisons between you and your older brother? Is that correct?")

o   When it appears the speaker is done, ask, "Is there more?"

The purpose of repeating back what the other person says is to be sure you are hearing him/her accurately. This requires you as the listener to put your ideas and responses on hold. Validate the other person, letting him know that you really see and understand his point of view. Although the individual's opinion differs from yours, acknowledge the validity of his thoughts. Typical validation phrases might include: "That makes sense…" or "I can see that because…" or "I can understand that because…"

To be an effective listener, seek to understand and to make the speaker feel understood. Becoming a professional listener will allow your teens to gain comfort and confidence in their relationship with you. And it will increase your influence with them because you will gain their trust, their attention, and their permission to respond.

The Importance of Respect

"You're just a child. I've been living much longer than you have, and I know much more than you do."

"Wait until you become my age and then try to come talk to me about your opinion…"

"You're just 16 years old, and I am a grown man."

"You don't need to know why. You wouldn't understand anyway. Do it because I said so!"

Often, when people discuss respect concerning parent-teen relationships, they are emphasizing the importance of the teen respecting the parent. It is absolutely true that when children do not honor their parents, they hinder many blessings in their lives (e.g. Exodus 20:12, Ephesians 6:1, Colossians 3:20). It is the order of God that parents are the authority figures and the physical and spiritual covering for their kids. For that, they should be honored.

● ● ●

To be an effective listener, seek to understand and to make the speaker feel understood.

● ● ●

However, you cannot control others, but you can control yourself. What you do as the parent makes a tremendous difference in the response of your teens. As much time as people spend rebuking kids for their disrespect, disrespect is still blatant and rampant among today's teens, particularly American youth.

Let's try something a little different and think about how you can influence their behavior. There are more scriptures about children obeying their parents, but take a look at what *else* the Bible says about the parent-child relationship…

In Ephesians 6:4 (NLT), the Bible states: "Fathers, do not provoke your children to anger by the way you treat them. Rather, bring them up with the discipline and instruction that comes from the Lord."

Therefore, God is teaching parents that you do not have to provoke your teens to anger in order to discipline them. God commands parents to discipline their children, but the "how" is important, just as the "what" is important. Thus, parents should not abuse their authority, using it as justification to mistreat their teens.

Many parents say, "Teens will be teens," and they expect certain misconduct from all teenagers, including their own! The truth is, parents actually don't have to accept the foolishness by treating them like hooligans. When parents respect their teens, they welcome more respectful behavior.

As youth pastors who have been leading our peers in ensembles, classes, services, and events since we were fifteen years old, we have only been blatantly disrespected by a few out of hundreds of youth we have worked with.

Why, if teenagers are such disrespectful and rebellious creatures, have they been able to respect our authority even though we are females who are a lot younger than their parents?!

We've carried ourselves with authority, respect, and kindness. We've treated them like they are mature adults simply working together, and they've acted like it!

Likewise, as we mention in the "Powerful Language" chapter, our parents treated us with so much respect that we were offended when other adults treated us like dumb, bad kids! We felt hurt! We could then understand why our peers acted the way they did, if that is how they were treated. Sometimes, people draw out of you certain behavior by the way they treat you.

Imagine, if someone disrespects a grown man by making him wear a bib every time he eats. He might eventually be a little less careful with his food. "Well, I have to keep wearing this ridiculous bib whether I eat neatly or not. Shoot! It doesn't even matter anymore..."

What about an innocent person being harassed by a police officer? That person's attitude often doesn't remain pleasant, and some even retaliate! If one is treated like a criminal, he might start acting like one. In fact, it could be in self-defense that the person becomes guilty of resisting an officer or PARENT.

Handling your teens like they're already guilty is never healthy for their self-image, morale, or future conduct. Of course, to the parent's defense, this approach is often due to previous misconduct of the teen, which resulted in broken trust.

Even the adults who treated us like "all the other mischievous teenagers" probably had so many negative experiences with teens that they assumed that all youth were irresponsible, rebellious, dishonest, and immature. This would explain why they treated us like we were beneath them, knowing nothing about us but our age.

Although it makes sense that more precautions would be taken after trust has been broken, you should never make your teens feel like they are "guilty until proven innocent."

If you treat them like bad kids, they start to believe they are bad kids, and they feel like their good deeds don't matter. If, at the end of the day, they are still punished as "bad kids," they will consequently behave like bad kids.

You might not have started the negative cycle, but you can certainly perpetuate it if you treat them according to the behavior that you don't like.

In fact, when you disrespect your teens and make them feel like their opinion is unimportant because they haven't lived as long as you have, you are actually accepting immaturity. You are validating it by your low expectations and by treating them like they are already irresponsible (See "Productive Mind Games" in section 1 of "Powerful Language").

Think about it: if you disrespect your teen, just like if you disrespect anyone, you trigger retaliation, and you model the very behavior that you don't want them to manifest.

Always remember that the best way to welcome respect is not to be harsh but is to be respectable!

We can remember talking to our mom in a disrespectful tone and feeling almost instant remorse because she responded with such respect and grace, even though that's not what we dealt to her. **Human nature seeks to reciprocate whatever is given—revenge for offense, friendliness for kindness, and respect for respect.**

If you feel like you're being disrespected, yelling, name-calling, and accusations can certainly backfire. Now, you have stooped to the level of your teen and lost his respect. Show your teens the better way by modeling maturity.

It was always very easy to respect our father because he carried himself in such a respectable manner. He never called us names, cursed at us, or belittled us. With distinction, grace, and class, he corrected us in eloquent, memorable ways. Dad encouraged us, supported us, and challenged us to live like leaders.

Walk what you talk and live what you preach. As we've said, you teach what you know, but you reproduce who you are. If you want them to respect your rule that profanity is not permitted, do not use profanity. **You demonstrate what you value by the way that you live.**

If you want them to control their temper, control yours. You shouldn't be yelling at them so loudly that your veins are protruding, your skin is reddening, your saliva is flying, and your eyes are bulging, while you're telling them to calm down and speak to you with respect.

Dr. Tommy Barnett confirms this truth as he titles the principle for one of his chapters in *The Power of the Half Hour* the following: **"Build character in children by showing them yours."**

When our entire family was on a panel at a conference discussing family, we were very interested to see what our brother would say. He was a junior in college at the time, and he wasn't the emotionally expressive type.

Consequently, he wasn't as open with our parents about his personal life as the rest of us were, at least to our knowledge. They did know his girlfriend, and she spent time with the family often. He even had extensive conversations with our parents often. Nevertheless, he was extremely private about his feelings and personal business.

What he said on this panel was brief because it was a school day, and he had to rush to class. But, it was sincere, and we even saw Dad's eyes watering (with no lint in it 😊).

He said that he didn't go completely wild and reject the church, like many other pastors' kids, not because he didn't have temptation, but because he had such immense respect for our parents. He said they lived their lives so authentically, remaining consistent inside and outside of the church, and making time to spend with him, that

> *You demonstrate what you value by the way that you live.*

even when he didn't always agree, how could he not respect their character?

Wouldn't you love for this to be said of you? It might not be said, but it can definitely become impressed upon your teen's heart when you live your life in a respectable manner before them and also show them respect.

Whatever It Takes

Just as our brother was much more private and less verbally expressive than his sisters, your teens will have noticeably different personalities. And, therefore, they will respond differently to exactly the same approach.

Some kids will answer your questions, like we and our sisters did with our mom. And, some will think that most of the questions are invasive and feel too private to share, like our brother did at times.

On the other hand, our brother-in-law is private and somewhat reserved, but he shared most of his private life with his mom.

The point is that some personality types require more strategic effort to delve into the details of their lives. And even still, some might never be as verbally expressive about their feelings and relationships as others.

Realistically speaking, your teen might not be the most talkative or the most eager to open up. You might even have walls to break down that might have been constructed through ridicule by peers, molestation by a relative, abandonment by your spouse, or even harsh words from you.

Sometimes, professional counseling for the family is needed in order to open the lines of communication. Be determined that despite the cost, regardless of how time-consuming or expensive, you will seek restoration of intimacy through healthy communication.

Be aware that some churches offer counseling free of charge, and some are connected with centers or schools that provide professional counseling for free (Our church offers both!).

Regardless of the attitude of your teens, they always long for your attention, even if they resist your initial efforts toward improvement. You never know what your teens are dealing with internally that might've caused their negative attitude towards you or towards life. Don't take it personally, allowing offense to hinder healing. **Listen intently, and let love lead you.**

Friend AND Parent

With open communication, active listening, respect, integrity, healthy boundaries, and persistence, we can bridge the gap between parent and teen.

Remember that the goal is to cultivate the kind of relationship with your teens in which they respect your authority *and* feel comfortable sharing the details of their lives with you.

That way, **you can do your job as a parent with the inside information of a friend.** Any job is performed better with deeper knowledge, and parenting is no different.

Being a parent who holds both "parent" status (respect, authority, and influence) and "friend" status (transparency, acceptance, and accountability) doesn't mean you're passive or immoral. And it doesn't mean you're trying to be your teen's best friend.

It means that you discipline in love and give them the freedom to share with you versus hide from you; to talk *with* you versus just listen *to* you; and to live *with* you and not just under your roof. Thus, you have the access of both friend and parent, the best position to know them and grow them.

● ● ●

Remember that the goal is to cultivate the kind of relationship with your teens in which they respect your authority and feel comfortable sharing the details of their lives with you.

● ● ●

CHAPTER 5
T-I-M-E

Terrance: "Where were you, Dad? It was the biggest game of the season. Everyone else had their parents cheering for them but me."

Recitals, sports games, graduations, birthdays, performances, births, housewarmings, promotion celebrations, weddings— whether young or old, your children crave your support. **Emotional support is vital, but demonstrating that support by yielding your time is priceless.**

There's no gift you can purchase to make up for your absence, and nothing can fully erase the memory of their special moment when you weren't there. You know, like that time when they excitedly looked out in the audience and did NOT see your face... You cannot afford to miss special moments in your teen's life, meaning that you should make your presence a non-negotiable. Make it such a priority that only emergencies can interfere.

When reminiscing over his dad's life at the funeral, this tall teenage son passionately expressed gratitude for his dad's attendance at every sports game he ever played. With tears in his eyes, he said something like the following: "My dad never missed one of my games. It meant the world to know that he was always there. I'm gonna miss him so much."

How do you want to be remembered in your kids' minds and hearts? As the parent who meant well but was just too busy? Or as the parent who was always there no matter what?

Support your teens in a way that convinces them you care even without words. **Your presence will teach them their importance to you.** To the busy parents out there, your teen feels even more special when you show up. Then he knows he is more important than your to-do list.

Our parents have always been busy people, particularly our father. Having him at every recital, graduation, book launch party, and birthday has always been beyond meaningful. Despite the countless important components of his daily schedule, we always manage to make it on his calendar when it counts.

As we were growing up, our father intentionally declined many speaking engagements that would cause him to travel excessively and be absent too often from home. He made sure he could be there for us, even if it meant forfeiting thousands of dollars.

Our mother has attended everything we have been a part of, no matter how trivial. If you didn't want her to show up, you just couldn't tell her about it. Haha! Watching her smiling face in the audience and hearing her exaggerated encouragement at the end always made us feel like a million bucks, even if we originally thought we sucked.

As busy as our father was, he definitely couldn't make every little thing for his five kids, but he always made a way for the important things. He didn't miss the major events that were meaningful to us.

Even if he never gave us gifts or encouraging words (which he did), his presence has always shown us that we are important to him. Because of his corresponding actions, his words and gifts were always well-received.

Sometimes kids have a hard

* * *

Your presence will teach them their importance to you.

* * *

time understanding you love them when you don't show up for their significant life moments. **Money, apologies, and compliments simply cannot substitute your time.** Those things become trite and meaningless when not coupled with your presence. As much as teens want to understand your busy schedule with their head, your excuses cannot reach their heart.

There is only one time that we can remember when our parents failed to show up at something important in our lives, and we didn't before realize how disappointed and hurt we would feel. Imagine how much worse it is when you miss *many* moments!

In this instance, our parents were scheduled to be in Singapore during the same weekend of our annual Christmas Carol Concert with the Spelman College and Morehouse College glee clubs. This concert was a very big deal, and we had spent the entire fall semester preparing for it.

After all of the long rehearsals that extended into the school's study period for final exams, we were disheartened by our parents' schedule conflict. We tried to understand that they had their trip planned long ago, but logic couldn't eradicate our disappointment.

Even though we knew ahead of time that they wouldn't be there, it was saddening to look into the audience after all of our hard work and never see their proud faces. While the other students were greeting their parents afterwards, we felt the sting of their absence.

We then understood what too many teens endure on a regular basis when their parents fail to support them in important moments.

Because of the love, admiration, and respect that kids tend to have for their parents, your support is irreplaceable. Teens naturally crave your approval and desire for you to be proud of them, even in college! How can you rave about their performance if you weren't there to see it? In order for you to be emotionally present for them in the most effective way, you must be physically present.

Boundaries

We will never forget this notable story highlighting the priorities of a very prominent motivational speaker...

When asked to speak to an audience of several thousands for a price of $10,000 or more, he declined. What an offer! Public speaking was his passion, and he loved his job. Although he was flattered by the offer, he confidently chose to spend the evening in pajamas, bonding with his family over a movie.

Choices like these don't come easily unless your commitment to your priority outweighs your passion for the other opportunity. This man had already committed to spending that time with his family; thus, instead of acting like a workaholic, he decided to keep his word and act like the family man he desired to be.

The truth is, you will always have something important on your to-do list. Don't allow your career or even charitable missions to be sufficient excuses to neglect your family. **Unfortunately, excuses don't raise healthy teens.**

Pastor Jeanne Mayo made a powerful statement of priority that went something like this: "In life, you will always juggle many balls. Only some of those balls are made of glass. Your family is one of them, and you cannot afford to drop it."

As busy as she is leading her youth pastors' mentoring program (Cadre), directing the Atlanta Leadership College, writing books, speaking around the world, running a large youth ministry, and too much more to mention, she has made the life-altering decision to keep her family as a top priority in her life.

To support her decision, she has a limit for the number of speaking engagements that she will accept per month. No matter what opportunity she is offered, she respects her designated limit. In fact, she has declined speaking for world-renown conferences more than once because she had already reached her limit of engagements for the month. Wow, what a dedicated mom!

Every parent must create boundaries. **Limit your work so it can come this far and no further.** That way, you leave space to nurture your most important priority after God—your family. For those in full-time ministry or any non-profit organization, remember that your family is your first ministry. **So don't use "serving others" as an excuse to fail at your mission to your spouse and your kids.** If everyone focused on raising their own healthy family, much of the work of these organizations would be done.

● ● ●

Don't neglect the important for the seemingly urgent.

● ● ●

Remember that failure to plan is a plan for failure, so you can't just let life happen to you, but you have to tell it how to go! You could have amazing intentions and one day realize that you have neglected the very thing that matters the most. **Don't neglect the important for the seemingly urgent.** There will always be something to do.

At the end of your life, your trophies won't matter, only people will. Your legacy lives through people, not material things that will rust and rot. People will reflect on the impact that you had on their lives, not on your accomplishments. So don't let your family be the ball you drop.

Clear Time Benefits

Several articles say the same things about family time, meaning we should pay attention. Quality time with your kids produces the following benefits[1]:

1. Improves child's academic performance
2. Reduces chance of substance (drugs/alcohol) abuse
3. Strengthens family bond
4. Helps kids develop parenting skills (They learn from your example!)
5. Reduces instances of behavioral problems
6. Lessens violence
7. Improves self-esteem
8. Boosts social skills

---

[1] Paolicchi, Scarlet (2015, May 8). "10 Important Benefits of Family Time" [Web blog post]. *Family Focus Blog*. Retrieved from http://familyfocusing.com

Additionally, a study[2] that was done on 200 people over 7 years showed that teenagers who spend more time with their parents have better social skills and higher self-esteem. Parents often fail to realize just how important this time issue is to their home. Sometimes teenagers' behavior can be confusing: when you're around, they have their earphones in, they text excessively, or even seem to be ignoring you. Certain behaviors are just normal for teenagers and don't mean what you think they do. It's a "cool" thing for them to pretend like they don't care, but they actually DO!

Additionally, more and more studies are discovering that teens spending time with their father, in particular, is especially crucial to boosting their social confidence and self-esteem.[3] This doesn't mean that the mother's role is less important. Understand that most families have mothers who are active in the home, but the father's role is not usually as consistent. When the father is just as active in the home, the outcome for the kids is significantly healthier.

With this in mind, strongly consider spending more quality time with your kids. And make sure that mother and father are involved in this commitment. If you (the parents) are not married, rise above your differences, and make sure both parents are regularly investing quality time with the kids. If one parent is out of the picture, invite a mentor (who shares your values) to fulfill the role of the missing parent. However it looks for your family, make sure that mother and father figures are spending regular quality time with the kids so they can be their best.

---

[2] Cohen, Tamara (2012, August 21). "No, really… talk to your teenager: Those who spend more time with their parents have better social skills". *Mail Online*. Retrieved from http://www.dailymail.co.uk.com

[3] Gray, Barbara B. (2012, August 21). "Teens Benefit by Spending More Time with Parents". *U.S. News and World Report*. Retrieved from https://health.usnews.com

Intentional Memory-Making

Mexico, Australia, Costa Rica, England, Italy, and the list goes on... Our parents have always scheduled annual family vacations that have given us memories of a lifetime!

We'll never forget the excursions we took in Costa Rica when our family went ziplining in the lush, green forest; when we slid down a concrete waterslide in the middle of that forest, wearing funny-looking helmets as we glided on the ice-cold river water; and when we ate enough rice and beans to last us a year!

From horseback riding at sunset on the beach to dancing the night away on a family-friendly party boat to swimming with dolphins, what teen could forget the family bonding that happens with strategic effort and financial investment from mom and dad?

Most parents who have five children would enjoy the world, as a couple, while their kids complain at home with the baby-sitters. On the contrary, our parents not only took us with them sometimes, but they also planned and continue to plan vacations specifically with the whole family in mind.

We understand that not everyone has the finances to take several kids with them out of the country, but you can get creative and be intentional about making family memories together. It might be in your budget to travel only within your country or even within your state. Do what you can, and make it memorable!

If you find that no travel accommodations are affordable enough for your family, plan something at home or at a friend's house. For young kids, you can do things like setting up little tents, flashlights, and s'mores in the backyard.

When we were kids, we set up a sheet across our twin beds and put heavy household objects on the beds to hold the sheet up—and wah la! We had our own homemade tent that we invited our brother to enjoy with us for days! We got flashlights and this tiny black and white picture TV that we found lying around somewhere. Inside the tent, we watched black and white TV (even though we had color TVs downstairs!), played games, ate, told stories, and slept. We didn't want to leave! As parents, you can create these kinds of economical, fun experiences for your young kids.

For teenagers and above, you can plan occasional family game nights and movie nights with their favorite meals and snacks. You can even put up decorations for it and blast music through the house. Make it an event! We have hilarious memories from family game nights with outrageously wrong answers and bad acting! We even still laugh remembering Mom screaming at the television and then crying during the film at our movie nights.

For older ones who love to dance, you can host random parties with family and friends or even bonfires in the backyard.

You can plan special themes, like Mexican night with tacos, salsa dancing lessons from YouTube, and a piñata. Or you can even create their favorite superhero night with a movie marathon and trivia questions. The possibilities are endless! All you need is an imagination to create memorable moments. If you don't consider yourself a creative person, ask your most creative friends and even your teens for ideas.

If you do have the money to spend on exotic vacations, then remember that it's well worth it. Your teens will benefit from the exposure they receive through traveling, and they'll have exciting stories to tell forever. Traveling helps them to be more globally minded as they see for themselves that the world is bigger than their own state or country.

Most importantly, though, create positive memories that will strengthen your family's bond and show your teens that you genuinely enjoy their company. After all, you don't want the main thing they remember about their time with you to be your yelling about the dishes!

The Power of *Table Time*

Our family has always made time for at least one meal together per week, even after all of us grew up and moved out! There is something very valuable about family time around the table.

As kids, we had family dinner every night. Because we come from a family of seven, the family naturally became too busy for a daily dinner time together. Between such activities as choir practice, SAT prep classes, and basketball practice, it became impractical to expect that our schedules would align every day.

> ● ● ●
>
> *Despite the sacrifice, never minimize the power of what can happen around the table.*
>
> ● ● ●

Consequently, we began reserving Tuesday nights and Sunday afternoons for our family dinners. These were times when we would talk about current events, positive news, dating relationships, funny stories from the week, exciting updates about other people's lives, hilarious jokes, serious issues that needed prayer, and a multitude of other topics. This table time kept us all abreast of each other's lives.

Still, as adults, we make it our point to cherish Sunday afternoon meal times and reserve them for family. Even if we are exhausted after church and the family plans to meet an hour away from where we live (since we are all scattered around the city), we are committed to attend anyway because we value it. Afterwards, we often have to drive an hour home in heavy traffic; but it's all worth it for the investment in our family bonds that are more important than how our bodies feel at the moment.

Despite the sacrifice, never minimize the power of what can happen around the table.

Time Tips

There are simple ways you can incorporate quality time with your teens in everyday life. As you read the list below, take note of the ones you plan to implement:

1. Errands: Take your teens with you as you run certain errands. You'll be surprised how far these little moments can go in your relationship.

2. Dates[4]: Plan individual dates with your teens. This doesn't have to be anything that you do often; but every now and then, take just one of your kids out and give him your undivided attention as well as the freedom to choose the location. It could be a lunch date, dinner date, or even a date to the park where you pack sandwiches and his favorite candy bar!

3. Family vacations: Do whatever fits your budget, but make it special! It could be a road trip, something overseas, something annual, or every other year. Just do your best.

4. Meal times: Eat as many meals with your family as possible, and ask detailed questions to remain engaged in everyone's world.

5. Extra-curricular activities: Be intentional about attending every game, recital, etc. Put it on your calendar and come ready to cheer!

6. Cell phone: Emphasize to them that you're never too busy for them and that they have the freedom to call or text you anytime. Of course, it might be impossible for you to answer sometimes, but make sure they know they can contact you and leave a voicemail or text. And do your best to respond quickly.

7. Their interests: Do things with your teens that you know they're interested in. Whether it's your favorite or not, give it a shot and get involved with them (e.g. video games, sports in the backyard, shopping, dancing, board games). Let them teach you something new, something they enjoy.

8. Electronics: Increase the quality of your time with your teens by turning off all electronics (yours and theirs!) during designated times. You could start with maybe one hour per week where you spend time

---

[4] Klassen, Dave with Hoos, Glen (2003). "10 Ideas: Creating Quality Time with Your Kids". *Family Life*. Retrieved from http://www.familylife.com

together with no electronics, and see where it goes from there. You might choose to increase the time without electronics when you notice the greater depth in your conversation as a result. (You might want to try going on walks together, playing board games, or even just sitting and talking on the couch.)

9. New things[5]: You can bond with your teens by teaching them new things like how to cook or how to change a tire. These are skills that they will appreciate in life, and you can make memories together in the process.

10. Family night: Schedule nights where the whole family comes together to do fun activities and create memories. These family nights can be spent at home with movies, games, conversation, and food, or they can be spent out at the bowling alley, a movie theater, or even on a biking trail.

The Charge

Teens might not articulate their values as well as you do, but they definitely know what they feel. Aside from what your family looks like on paper, what does it feel like to them? Does it feel genuine, passionate, loyal, and heartfelt? Only time can yield this kind of fruit that not only looks good, but tastes ripe and brings health and wholeness to the family.

Be determined to go out of your way to spend quality time with your spouse and kids, and make it meaningful. If you need fresh ideas, you can google to discover what some other families are doing with each other! Simply, never give up.

When your actions speak louder than your words do, make sure that's a beautiful message.

[5] Morin, Amy (2017, June 19). "10 Ways to Spend Quality Time with Your Teen". *Very Well Family*. Retrieved from https://www.verywellfamily.com

When your actions speak louder than your words do, make sure that's a beautiful message. Prove to your teens how much you love them through T-I-M-E, quantity and quality.

CHAPTER 6

TEENS IN THE SPOTLIGHT

What It's Like

While sitting in a parenting session taught by our parents at our father's 2014 Capacity Conference, we heard Dad's words on this subject that we couldn't have said better ourselves:

"It is all too common for the children of great men to grow up to be very ordinary despite their genetic inheritance or to have serious problems living up to the famous name they inherited. Sometimes, the father casts so large a shadow that he makes it hard for his children to find the sunshine they need to grow and flourish."

He also shared the thoughts of kids who were born to very prestigious parents.

Nelson Mandela's daughter is quoted saying to him, "You are the father of all our people, but you never had the time to be a father to me."

Eleanor Roosevelt once shared the sorrowful insight that "a man in high public office is neither husband nor father nor friend in the commonly accepted meaning of those words."

Albert Einstein's son Hans, who went on to have a

> • • •
>
> *Too often, parents in the spotlight are so preoccupied with their career success that they neglect their familial success.*
>
> • • •

distinguished career as a scientist, sadly commented, "The only project my father ever gave up on was me."

What a shame that you could seemingly help the world, yet lose your own home, the very people that God originally entrusted to you!

Yes, your teens get a lot of attention because of their last name, but are they getting it from you? It's no wonder that the offspring of influential people don't always turn out as great or powerful as their parents. **Too often, parents in the spotlight are so preoccupied with their career success that they neglect their familial success.**

If your nanny or the TV spends more time with your kids than you do, whom do you expect them to become more like? Teens in the spotlight can become great by spending time around greatness—YOU.

The "Spotlight"

Not every teen knows what it feels like to have parents who are in the spotlight, but teens who are in this position know that it is a unique struggle. We define "parents in the spotlight" as those in influential positions in their career who have come to prominence.

Actor, news anchor, model, entrepreneur, pastor (our case), athlete, musician, politician—whatever your profession, if large groups of people take notice of you, you're "in the spotlight." Because of the abundance of attention that these kinds of parents attract, people take special interest in their kids… hence, "teens in the spotlight."

Imagine the amount of pressure it places upon people, knowing that others will notice their every move. The world has watched as numerous celebrities have crumbled under these conditions, falling prey to drugs, alcohol, depression, and more. How much worse could this be for the unprepared mind of a child?

Although this celebrity example is an extreme case, the basic principle is true: It is very unhealthy to strip human beings of their right to be human and make mistakes like everyone else. And when people are watching your every move, they will see these mistakes.

When we were freshmen in college, we made only one embarrassing grade, which we clearly remember because we were completely exposed by our professor! In front of the whole class he blurted, "Wow! Bishop Bronner's daughters failed my quiz! I can't believe this. I should tell your father."

Who would have guessed that he would give us a detailed quiz about his life (i.e. his undergraduate and graduate institution, his academic societies, etc.) on the second day of class?!

Needless to say, we both failed the quiz, along with the majority of the class. No one else was individually rebuked for her failing grade; but, as usual, there was special treatment for the "teens in the spotlight."

On the first day of class, this particular teacher randomly said in front of everyone something like, "Well, well, well... It's the Bronner sisters! I know who you two are. I know your family business and your father's church. Who doesn't know the Bronners in Atlanta? I'm sure you two will be straight A students."

We were straight A students after that first quiz, but not because we had something to prove to him! We laughed about the experience when we left the classroom, but it was a bit embarrassing.

Before moving on, we must acknowledge that there are obvious perks and privileges of being a teen in the spotlight. As PKs (a.k.a. pastor's kids), there's VIP treatment, automatic recognition and respect, a sense of pride in who your parents are, and more opportunities.

The perks definitely make a kid feel special. But, we must focus on the part that many people fail to notice—the all-too-common pressures and struggles of a teen in the spotlight.

Although parents cannot stop others from approaching their kids with foolish questions or comments, parents in the spotlight should be careful to do what they can to nurture their teen's emotional health. In this chapter, we will highlight the struggles of teens in this position so that you are aware and equipped to care for their needs.

Our Story

"Wow, you girls are very well-behaved. My husband and I were watching you two and your friends during the movie, and your parents would be very proud! Are these gentlemen your boyfriends?... If I get the chance to speak with your father up-close, I will let him know about your wonderful behavior!"

What an invasion of our personal lives to have strangers monitoring us in the movie theater! As teenagers, when we went to the theater, mall, a restaurant, or any other recreational facility in Atlanta (our home city), we often had encounters like this one with people whom we did not recognize.

Our "spotlight" comes from our father's role as senior pastor and founder of a megachurch, one of the fastest growing churches in America. The services stream live and broadcast around the world. Although the church was not always the 20,000-member operation that it currently is, we have always received a lot of attention because we are PKs.

In addition, our father is one of the Bronners of the Bronner Bros. hair care company. Everywhere we go in Atlanta (the home of the church and family business), people recognize us as "Bishop Bronner's daughters" or ask us, "Bronner, as in the Bronner Brothers hair products?"

Growing up, people asked us a lot of questions. Although we were often approached in public, most of the questions came from people at church. When you go to a megachurch, that means questions from many people you don't know in addition to those you know.

The questions at church, besides the ridiculous twin ones, typically sounded something like this: "What grades are you making in school?" "Do you have a boyfriend?" "What do you want to be when you grow up?" "You don't do the crazy stuff that the rest of these teens are doing, do you?" Everyone wanted to know our personal business and whatever inside story they could get on our lives, whether they had a relationship with us or not.

Our parents would sometimes tell us things like, "Mrs. Johnson told us today that she saw you girls at the mall, and she said that you're the most respectable and well-behaved young ladies that she's ever seen! She told us that we've done such a great job raising you two, and that we should be some extremely proud parents."

The good part about reports like this one was that it gave our parents nice compliments and assured them that we were responsible even when they weren't looking. The downside to these reports was that we felt like we were being watched! Who wants to feel like you're under surveillance when you're goofing off with your friends?

"Aww man, I wonder if she saw us making those ridiculous facial expressions while we were joking around with Sarah?! She might have thought we were seriously about to hit her! Wow, that's embarrassing!"

When teens are just being teens, it's invasive to have people scrutinizing their every move. Additionally, knowing that people were reporting our behavior to our parents, we felt the need to keep our behavior, even our silliness, presentable at all times. There are certain things you trust only your friends and family to see.

Whether we recognized people or not, we knew there was a great chance they recognized us. We learned that, when we saw random adults smile or nod, it usually meant they knew we were "Bishop Bronner's daughters." To this day, we sometimes accidentally respond to a strange man's flirtatious smile and nod! This is because we've had too much practice greeting random people in public who MIGHT be members of our church... It gets confusing! Haha!

Now, let's clarify: we actually greatly enjoy being PKs. We grew up feeling special, and we had a lot of people praying for us, supporting us, and even giving us gifts though they didn't know us.

Sure, there were annoying parts. In fact, the most annoying stuff has always been the twin questions, jokes, and comparisons, which we get everywhere that we're together. But, at the end of the day, the church members are actually like our extended family. We appreciate their genuine love and kindness: they really are a major part of our lives.

Okay, now that we've made that disclaimer, here's another "con" to all the extra attention: One time when we were very shy pre-teens, a nasty rumor was spread about us among some of the youth at the church. The girl who started the rumor hated us from an early age without cause. She claimed that we, along with one of our other sisters, were so-called "closet freaks" (secretly promiscuous). We weren't too hurt because the rumor was far from the truth. We were virgins who had not even had our first kiss yet!

Another example is the notion that we were "stuck up" (haughty). Although there were others who were just as shy as we were, whispering to their own family members, we were the ones given this negative label. Just because of who our father was, we were apparently expected to be best friends with the whole church! In other words, we felt like they expected us to be outgoing and friendly to everyone. These were very high and unrealistic expectations for pre-teens too shy in public to even say, "I'm hungry"!

When you're in the spotlight, people *will* talk about you. It's just a fact. They will talk about you more than they talk about others. And, you might not be able to understand why. Plain and simple, **those in the spotlight are very conspicuous targets.**

Most people don't think about odd struggles like these, but that's why we're shedding light for those families who share the spotlight, in its blessings and its struggles.

Problems & Solutions

The Spotlight Struggle

T he average person has the option of keeping his/her sin hidden because not as many people are looking. For those in the spotlight, others eagerly note and spread every bit of dirt they can find.

It seems unfair when you think about it, but honestly, you can't change the natural nosiness of human beings. As a parent in the spotlight, the best you can do is prepare your teens specifically for this struggle.

Often, parents in the spotlight don't prepare their children because they were never teens in the spotlight themselves and perhaps never considered the issues that could arise.

Some of the challenges that parents of teens in the spotlight should consider are the following:

1. Lack of privacy
2. High achievement expectations from the parent
3. High achievement expectations from others
4. Unusual pressure (created by uncommon attention)
5. Annoying/offensive questions and comments from strangers
6. Gossip about the parent
7. Gossip about the teen
8. Responsibility to protect the parent's reputation
9. Difficulty making genuine friends (Many will be drawn by one's status.)
10. Lack of a "normal" childhood (realizing he/she will *always* be different)
11. Judgment or envy from others
12. Finding one's own identity aside from the parent's

We've already discussed some of these struggles, and others pretty much speak for themselves; however, we'll take a moment to expound upon a few key points.

Number 8—Responsibility to Protect the Parent's Reputation

Teens in the spotlight soon learn the importance of others' opinions. This can definitely incite bitterness and stir rebellion because it creates a box for teens to live in that's difficult to understand.

"Why is it other people's business what I do?" "I'm not living to please people I don't even know, so what's the point?!" These kinds of thoughts often plague the minds of teens in the spotlight.

With well-known reputations to protect, parents in the spotlight might respond more harshly to their teen's misconduct. This is because it's not just the reputation of the child on the line, but that of the parent(s).

It creates excess pressure for the teen when the parent says things like, "Now, don't go in there embarrassing me. People are watching you." Interestingly enough, teens can sense this type of attitude even when it's not specifically verbalized.

One teen in the spotlight disclosed the following: "My dad would fly home to spank my brother, and then fly back... Kids are good at picking up on their parents' behavior." This teen perceived his father's actions as more than just commitment to discipline. He believed his dad went over and beyond to protect his reputation that was connected to his son's.

The truth is that the parent obviously cared since he spent the time and money to fly home to correct his child. But apparently, this father needed to clarify his motive. **Your teen should always understand that you care more for his/her well-being than for your own reputation.**

Even though our parents did a great job of avoiding the parental pitfalls of this topic, we, too, struggled with our own version of "other people's opinions." Our mother would often quote the scripture, "Abstain from all appearance of evil"—1 Thessalonians 5:22.

She explained that, even if you're not doing anything wrong, if it *looks* bad, avoid it. Your reputation can be tainted just as

● ● ●

Your teen should always understand that you care more for his/her well-being than for your own reputation.

● ● ●

much by what people *thought* you did as by what you *actually* did.

For example, teenagers often engage in all types of sexual immorality in the dark on the back rows of movie theaters and buses. Consequently, we weren't allowed to sit on the back rows of these places. It was clear that she trusted our character but simply didn't want others to see us coming out from the shadows and make false assumptions.

Although we obeyed, we did complain about her restrictions. We had a hard time understanding why we couldn't have the freedom to sit wherever we wanted to, especially since she knew we weren't troublemakers and we were committed virgins.

It was embarrassing to explain to our friends why we had to strain our necks looking up at the close theater screen because the only *good* seats left were on the back row. And, yes, we also might have wanted to kiss our boyfriends without church members watching!

We felt compelled to pay attention to our surroundings at all times and remain aware of who might be watching us, whether we recognized them or not.

Although her rules were inconvenient for us, it was good advice. The Bible does say, "Choose a good reputation over great riches..." (Proverbs 22:1a NLT). Also, how can you represent Jesus well if your personal reputation is not respected?

We later understood and embraced all of her logic. We can only imagine how much worse our attitudes would've been if she instead said things like, "Don't embarrass me or your father!" or "Be on your best behavior because you carry the Bronner name!"

Instead, both of our parents reminded us of the following

truth: The only opinions that matter are these three—1) your opinion of yourself, 2) God's opinion of you, and 3) your opinion of God. "You are living to please God and representing Jesus everywhere you go," they would say.

Their method definitely reduced our desire to rebel and inspired us to care about how we represented Jesus instead of just pleasing people.

Number 9—Difficulty Making Genuine Friends

As a "privileged" teen in general, people try to get close to you just because of your last name or what they perceive you have to offer. Often, these people don't care about how well your personality blends with theirs. They simply want the "perks" of being your friend.

Some seek validation for their identity through their association with you. It makes them feel popular, exclusive, and important to be your friend because not everyone gets that opportunity. They like to enter the VIP areas with you, occupy front-row seats with you, and come see what your house looks like on the inside.

A couple of so-called "friends" we had always tried to persuade us to sit on the front row at church, just so they could sit down there with us. They enjoyed people asking, "Who are those girls that sit with you down front all the time?"

We actually didn't like to sit in the front because we felt uncomfortable with the bright lights and all the attention that we received. We didn't even realize at the time that they were enjoying the perks of our privileges a bit too much.

Additionally, when we had a group of teens over our house, some of them went back to church bragging about their experience and describing in detail what our house looked like.

It's definitely difficult to trust people's motives when, so often, they take great pleasure in proving to others how well they know you. "You know, she and I hang out all the time. I go over her house like every weekend." When your peers use statements like these to boast to others, you're left to question the purity of their intentions in the friendship.

A guy friend we invited to our house later bragged saying, "I saw Bishop chillin' with a sandwich!" Our family always laughed about this one. How ridiculous that something so little was significant to that guy just because of our dad's status!

Honestly, human nature takes pride in its associations of high status even if the people do genuinely love you. The problem is that, too often, those who enjoy your perks too much don't unconditionally accept you. You must wonder, "If I weren't the mayor's kid, would Jeremy still hang out with me every weekend?"

These people who are preoccupied with the authority of your name and the luxury of your possessions are the same ones who allow their hearts to go lusting after everything that belongs to you.

When people want what you have, it's not long before their attitudes and actions reveal self-advancement rather than concern for your well-being. They are forever trying to get ahead, catch up with you, and live vicariously through you. It's simply unhealthy.

Sometimes, people behave differently around you because they are concerned about impressing you. The additional respect can be nice sometimes, but other times, it's just another load on the pile of what makes your life less "normal." When other teens don't feel the freedom to fully be themselves around you, it typically restricts you from being yourself around them.

We will never forget the times when we would walk up to a group of kids during what appeared to be a fun conversation, and they would awkwardly glance at us and get quiet. They'd then transition to a more mellow discussion that they thought was more appropriate for us to hear.

For some reason, people thought that we weren't normal kids! They'd sometimes ask us strange questions like, "Do you go to the movies?" "Do you talk on the phone?" "Do you hang out at the mall?"

Considering these frequent scenarios, genuine friendship can be a tremendous challenge for teens in the spotlight. Help your teens by providing wisdom and encouragement to choose the right friends despite the odds.

Number 11—Judgment or Envy from Others

Being a teen in the spotlight can appear very glamorous. People see all of the attention, money (typically), privileges, and opportunities, and they often feel like, "These kids are favored from birth without working for it." It appears that these teens are some sort of special heirs, and good things just naturally flow in their direction.

With this in mind, it is not uncommon for jealousy to arise. Unfortunately, some people assume that teens in the spotlight are spoiled brats, while others secretly desire to *be* them. Either perspective is unhealthy and can create negative experiences for your teens.

One teen in the spotlight shared her frustrations about a situation with her college professor. After the instructor had missed many days of class, she scheduled appointments with each student to negotiate their grades. An hour late for the meeting, the student panicked and raced to contact the teacher to apologize for her tardiness and to reschedule.

Instead of showing any mercy, the professor issued her an undeserved "D." To another faculty member, the instructor stated, "I will not do anything about this: I don't care *who* her dad is." Sadly, the student later expressed the following: "I could tell she thought she was teaching me a lesson." This negative experience was clearly due to the professor's sentiments about the girl's "privilege."

When we were around 10 years old, we noticed another little girl who always tried to copy everything we did. Coincidentally, she was a singer just like we were, and we were part of the same children's choir.

When we got a new leather jacket, she got one just like it. When we straightened our hair, she straightened hers. When we got new black purses (probably our first purses), she got one, too. We even started carrying a hot pink C.D. player that we got for Christmas, and she got the exact same one! Now, that's hard to miss!

Because of her attitude towards us, it was clear that her imitation of us was not because of admiration, but rather envy. Whenever we tried to hug her, she, in return, flashed an extremely disingenuous grin and gave us the kind of hug that makes you wonder if you stink!

If we ever saw her across the hallway with her best friend, she would intentionally put her nose in the air while looking the other way, even though her friend reciprocated our greeting.

We always wondered why she didn't like us when we never offended her. Little did we know, it was our very position that she wished were hers instead.

When we were 15, another young lady approached us at a birthday party, and we were appalled by her unapologetic candor. She forced her right index finger onto one of our foreheads while simultaneously smashing her left index finger on the forehead of the other twin. With the utmost boldness, she articulated the following words:

"I'ma come to your house in the middle of the night with a pistol and shoot you [both] in the forehead! I hate y'all. You know why? Because y'all are light-skinned with long hair, and you got money! That's why."

The truth is, she didn't know us well enough to know how much money our family had or the nature of our personalities because we were still extremely shy at that age. She assumed many things about us because she knew who our parents were.

What did we do to deserve these toxic attitudes from others? The answer is simple: we did nothing but be teens in the spotlight.

How did our parents help us with this? They prepared us for it. We didn't bring it up, but they specifically addressed it. Occasionally, they would say something like this: "You know that people will be jealous of you. They will envy you because of who you are, what you have, and even because you're so beautiful.

But you can't worry about that. Know who you are, love people anyway, kill 'em with kindness, and walk in the freedom of the truth."

Because we weren't surprised by this issue, we were able to identify the attitude for what it was so that we didn't feel bad because of others' envy. The understanding of what these people were feeling also helped us to determine in advance to be unusually kind to them. This helped to improve our relationships with others. We eventually won the heart of the girl at the party who threatened us!

Number 12—Finding One's Own Identity

Many teens in the spotlight would agree that one of the primary challenges is finding one's own identity, outside of who your parents are.

"How does it feel to have such big shoes to fill?"—We, along with numerous other teens in the spotlight, have been asked this question. It can certainly be difficult to live one's own life under this pressure from a multitude of outsiders. **You feel stuck in someone else's shadow, and yet still expected to make your own big move.**

Kid-to-parent comparisons can seemingly overwhelm the life of a teen in the spotlight. When asked what is the hardest thing about being a kid in the spotlight, this young guy responded with the following:

> *Coming into my own. Realizing I am not him, and I don't have to be him, and I don't need to try to be him. Realizing my own purpose and that I have my own purpose and destiny. That was quite a process. That followed me even past high school. I had made up for myself a responsibility to carry the torch. It was hard to realize that his life has nothing to do with mine in that sense…That we are totally separate entities.*

Notice what he said about realizing his own purpose and

relieving himself of the pressure to be his father. The goal is not to be his father, but to grow from his example and stand on his father's shoulders to fulfill his unique calling.

Also, note the following words (paraphrased) from a teen in the spotlight who's an aspiring actor:

"I've never been in an audition where they didn't ask me about my dad. I want to know I got the part off my own merit, not who he is… They always assume that I will be great when I walk into the room, greater than the average person. It strips from me the room to make mistakes like everyone else. He was a millionaire at 21, and I'm not that."

Both of these young people are expressing their need to walk in their own identity and not in the shadow of their parents.

Also note that the identity challenge is far more intense depending on the gender of the teen in comparison to the gender of the well-known parent. For example, a boy would feel more pressure to be like his prestigious father than he would if it were his mother in the spotlight.

Because our father was the one in the spotlight, we didn't experience the same kinds of challenging comparisons that our brother did. Considering this concept, parents should monitor the emotional and mental progress of their teens in a more strategic manner based upon gender. For example, our brother had more need for the occasional father-son talk about freedom to find confidence in his own path than we did.

Sometimes, teens in the spotlight feel pressure from their parents, sometimes from the public, and sometimes simply from their self-imposed standards. Parents should be sensitive to the pressure their teens face and support them accordingly. Take a look at the following statements from a young guy describing his feelings of intimidation that induced his self-imposed pressure:

"I've traveled with him and seen him around the world. He is great among greats. This was around the time [13-14 years old] when I put the pressure on myself like, 'You're supposed to be *that* one day!'"

Notice that it wasn't his father's fault that he felt this way. He did nothing but be great! Nevertheless, his son put pressure upon himself because of the standard he observed.

We've realized that many teens in the spotlight put pressure on themselves because they are comparing themselves now to the example of their parents 30 years beyond the teen's stage in life! Parents should be mindful to clarify that there's room for growth over time, so their teens don't feel pressure to be some overnight wonder. It's unrealistic to skip the process in order to hurry and match accomplished parents. Often, it took the parents, themselves, a very long time to build their legacy. But the teen is comparing himself to a work that has long been in progress.

I (Kristie) have even felt discouraged trying to live up to the example of my mother, who I view as superwoman! She is so mature and extraordinary that it almost doesn't seem feasible. But I've been reminded that she wasn't that way when she was my age. And, in fact, because of her example, I am further along at my age than *she* was at my age! Perspective is everything. And parents, you'd be wise to share this perspective, even if your teens don't tell you their feelings. Honestly, they typically won't.

Be proactive to help your kids with whatever might be plaguing their minds. Because they need confidence to be their personal best, it's very important not to leave them in a discouraged state.

Try asking specific questions to discover how your teens feel; alleviate the pressure by occasionally reminding them of their unique, God-given identity; give them the freedom to pursue their own passions; and support their chosen path.

When you show your support to your teens in whatever they choose to do (that isn't harmful, of course), it esteems them in a way that's difficult to explain.

It meant a lot to me [what my dad said] when I was doing this whole gaming thing... I was playing my [video] game at night, and he [dad] came in my room. I don't even think I had ever seen him that stern before, and he told me to get off [the video games] and go to sleep. The next day, he apologized and said, "If you want to do this gaming thing, I will support you all the way." That helped me in my process.

We do want to clarify that, in this scenario, gaming is in reference to professional gaming, earning money through competitions. This teen decided not to pursue professional gaming after his season of involvement, but his dad's support built his confidence for whatever he put his mind to do. He then knew that he could rely on his father for support and encouragement through just about anything.

The advice of this same young man to parents reads, "Make it clear that, whatever you do, we'll support you. You can be or do whatever you want to do. No one is depending on you to carry the torch."

This disclaimer is highly important to the teen's process of development. Now, this young man is making his father very proud. He was able to flourish in the presence of support with the absence of unhealthy pressure.

One teen gave this powerful tip for parents: **"Build their confidence in 'you *get* to be you.'"**

You'd be surprised at the impact of simple words on the development of your teen's identity. Concerning his childhood claim to follow in his father's footsteps, one guy expressed that he wished his parents had said, "It's okay if you change your mind."

This same guy got older and realized that, although he loved, respected, and admired his father, he wasn't destined to be his dad's business successor, as ideal as it sounded.

Another teen shared the following: "My parents would say, 'You can't choose who your mom or dad is. You can be your own person.' That was always comforting to me."

The truth is that there's nothing wrong with parents desiring

● ● ●

Help your teens find their identity through your support and encouragement of who they are, not who you are.

● ● ●

to pass the baton of their business or career to their kids. In fact, that's great! But, sometimes the pressure of forcing it upon teens makes them reject or resent it. Instead, give them the freedom to undergo their own process and encourage the gifts you see in them. Sometimes their talents, passions, and admiration for you lead them to choose a similar path anyway!

Our parents would sometimes say things like, "Whatever is in your heart to do, do it. Be who God has called *you* to be. Whatever you choose, you will succeed at it, and we will support you all the way." We just so happened to follow in their footsteps, even though we weren't forced to.

We were encouraged to excel in our passions, and we ended up attending our mother's alma mater; doing biblical teaching like our father (starting at 15 years old, while he started at 14!); and, teaching music ensembles in church like our mom.

In short, **help your teens find their identity through your support and encouragement of who *they* are, not who *you* are.**

The Spotlight Solution

When you raise your teens in the spotlight with wisdom, they can one day echo the words of the young man who said the following about his father's position:

"Now, it's more of an inspiration. He has tons of wisdom and is willing to help me in a bunch of different ways. It sets a high bar, and is now inspiring."

Through his father's encouragement, what was once a source of intimidation became an inspiration.

Another teen in the spotlight that had a positive relationship with his parents said the following: "[As a teen in the spotlight] You feel like greatness runs in your blood. It's something to be proud of."

As a well-known parent with children, you have two options: 1) Your teens can grow up bitter, rebellious, or just plain ordinary; or, 2) they can be GREAT and even exceed your life's success as they stand on the shoulders of giants.

Your success should be something your teens can appreciate because they have a strong foundation on which to build their future, and they have access to your wisdom and experience.

Although numerous teens in the spotlight are spoiled by some, judged and mistreated by others, and often neglected by the ones that matter to them the most (THEIR PARENTS), they can be healthy. You can prepare your teens for the issues, nurture their emotional health, consistently encourage them, and set them up for great success.

But you must pay attention! Often, parents in the spotlight are so focused on their own obstacles as a man or woman of high influence that they forget about the impact that their position has on their teen.

Our parents definitely helped us process our experience. Our mother's role was a very vocal one, occasionally asking us questions to discover our thoughts about the position we were born into. She would pick our brains and track our progress from time to time, making sure that, even if we said we were okay before, we were still doing well.

The following questions are samples of the kinds of things that Mom used to ask us, which you can consider utilizing:

Do you feel like you're under pressure?

Do you feel like *we* put pressure on you?

Do you feel like you can be yourself?

Do you feel free to express yourself?

Do you feel like you're "walking on eggshells" (fearful, awkward, uncomfortable)?

How do you feel being a _____ (e.g. pastor's, actor's) kid?

Do you feel the freedom to make mistakes?

Do you feel like Dad and I hold you to a standard that's too high?

Mom also frequently affirmed us by saying, "You know that I will love you no matter what, right? Nothing you can do will make me love you any more or any less."

Our dad's role was not as vocal, but it was reassuring and comforting just the same. He never put pressure on us to be a certain way, and he never made us feel like we had to fit a certain mold of the "model child" to make him look good.

He never said anything like, "Now y'all don't embarrass me when we go in here. Be on your best behavior because people are watching you." Dad never treated us like we were "kids in the spotlight": to him, we were always just his kids.

He didn't force us into certain positions, coerce us to attend specific colleges, or push us to pursue certain career paths.

Instead, he always pointed out every gift he saw in us and regularly encouraged us accordingly. He told us that he was proud of us and gave us warm, long hugs that communicated deep love and acceptance. And because of these things, we knew that his love was unconditional.

Also, he was very present in our lives, even though he traveled a lot speaking in various countries around the world. Although his time was in high demand, he made sure to give us as much of it as we needed.

We always knew that he followed the priority list that his father established, which was God first, family second, and business third. His values were apparent every time he cleared his schedule for our recitals, birthdays, family dinners, and anything else we invited him to. Whatever was important to us was also important to him.

Furthermore, he never broke a promise. Every time he gave his word that he would attend something we valued, he was there and on time. We knew that he was truly a man of his word.

He even paid attention to the seemingly "little" things, like not answering the phone during a family meal or any other family time. And he always maintained clear division between work and personal life. This amazing sense of balance spoke louder than words ever could. Without hesitation or regret, he consistently put us first.

We knew that we didn't just have a great man living in our house: We had a dad who valued his role as a fully devoted father and husband more than his other titles. The attention that our famous dad gave (and still gives) to his wife and children was the greatest spotlight we could ever ask for.

CHAPTER 7
DISCIPLINE THAT WORKS

5-4-3-2-1...The sound of a parent's countdown before the imminent confrontation...Discipline isn't fun, but it is always necessary. If you don't discipline your teens, society will do it for you. Prison, violence, suspension from school, and termination from jobs are just a few examples. The world will not be patient or merciful, but it will correct and judge faithfully.

Many parents have gotten discipline all wrong. They are doing what their parents did without considering the main goal. **The goal is not to make your teen suffer, cry, or beg for mercy; but the goal is character development.** In order to develop maturity, responsibility, and integrity, you must correct with love.

There are key principles to discipline that every parent must apply in order to achieve the desired results, but the objective must first be understood. In this chapter, we will clarify the goal of discipline, and we will share keys for improvement. In addition to these keys, we will discuss how to choose the best method of discipline for your teen's personality and how to approach discipline most effectively.

The Importance of Discipline

"Love says to give your kids the carrots and spinach instead of daily candy, so as to preserve the teeth, health, and life of your kids. Even if they beg for junk food only, love says to give what they need versus what they want, even before they fully understand." — Anonymous

Discipline is vital to the overall health of every individual. As I (Kirstie) mention in "Friend or Parent," I was surprised to find that one of my teenage mentees actually responded with gratitude when I bluntly corrected her. She let me know that my correction made her feel loved, like I truly cared. Although I gave her truth that hurt, she found a strange sense of warmth in it… something she felt like she wasn't getting from her mother.

Teens who do not receive enough discipline actually crave that expression of love. When you set boundaries for them and provide structure for their lives, they feel like you care about their safety and overall well-being.

Just to clarify, this does not mean that teens will always welcome your disciplinary tactics with a smile and a hug. Generally, they won't. And, if they do, you've probably reached the end of your disciplinary journey! Haha!

More commonly, they will be ungrateful, exuding a pretty nasty attitude. Discipline will make them feel angry and annoyed; but then, if they don't get it, they feel like you don't care! Complicated, right?! But such is life…

Realistically, it could take years for them to appreciate your boundaries and correction. The truth is, as rebellious as they might seem *with* your discipline, you don't want to find out what they'd be like *without* it.

One adolescent male from a middle class family admitted that his parents did not discipline him enough. He said his mom would just throw things out there sometimes like, "You shouldn't hang out with certain types of people," but she never followed up with questions about his friends.

His father had what he called a "rope," meaning you could do whatever you want as long as you stay within certain loose boundaries. For example, Dad wasn't asking where you were, as long as you were home by curfew. This teenager decided that he wanted to be a certain type of man, and in order to make that happen, he needed to discipline himself. So, he did. Most adolescents are not so wise.

One Christmas, a boy's parents realized how ungrateful he had become. Because they were alarmed by his sense of entitlement, they boldly retracted all of his gifts to teach him a lesson. They explained to him the importance of gratitude and humility in life.

They returned his gifts to him a few months later for his birthday when he could appreciate them much more. Although most parents wouldn't want to endure the consequences on Christmas Day of making such an unpopular move, these parents realized that developing their son's character was more important than his comfort or theirs in that moment.

To no surprise, all of their children say, "Thank you" and "I really appreciate it" more than any other family we know. One day, I (Kirstie) asked the mother how she got her family to be such grateful people. Her answer was something like "a lot of intentionality... It didn't just happen."

Likewise, our parents were intentional about discipline, even if they didn't feel like it. When we were kids, our mom used to always say, "This is going to hurt me more than it's going to hurt you..." right before she spanked us. Sometimes, she would actually be crying as she did so. Although we didn't understand why she continued despite the pain that she claimed it caused her, she explained that she disciplined us *because* she loved us.

Her compassion demonstrated that it was not out of frustration or anger that she spanked us, but because of her love that outweighed our comfort. It was about what she knew we *needed*, rather than what we *wanted*.

We are not saying you need to cry as you discipline your kids in order to prove your love. Some personalities are a bit more emotional than others. But, we are saying to **demonstrate your love through discipline, even when you don't feel like it.**

Keys to Effective Discipline

Whether you're giving a spanking or a lecture, there are certain factors that must remain constant in order for discipline to be effective. These factors include maintaining consistency, operating on principle, communicating the "why," customizing the method for the personality, and using strategic language for character development.

Consistency

Mom: "If you go to school one more time without your homework, you'll be grounded for a week!"

Son: [thoughts] "Last week, I didn't do my homework either, and she said the same thing… She'll forget. I'll be alright."

When threats become empty because you forgot, "caved in," or just didn't feel motivated once you weren't angry anymore, your efforts to discipline become weak and futile. You must be consistent.

Your teen should expect that negative consequences *always* follow negative actions. If they only *sometimes* follow negative actions, your teen does not have enough motivation to deter him/her from the behavior.

Additionally, parents of multiple children should beware of inconsistency with the youngest child. Many older siblings complain, "If I did that, oh, it was a sure spanking, but he [the youngest] could always get away with it! He can get away with stuff we [the older siblings] never could!"

● ● ●

Demonstrate your love through discipline, even when you don't feel like it.

● ● ●

Although parents feel a little tired or lazy with the last child, they have to make sure that the youngest one doesn't become the lazy, irresponsible, immature one.

This young adult's experience demonstrates the consequences of getting lazy with your youngest child. He was the youngest of five kids, and his older siblings were often asked to do his chores for him and even clean his room! This is what he had to say about it:

> *While in college and grad school, I had plenty of time to reflect on my upbringing since I was away from home... I felt like I was working harder than other people to play "catch up" because I was very underdeveloped in responsibility and self-discipline. When I was forced to do everything on my own, it made me realize how little responsibility I had growing up and how much my mom enabled me. She meant well, but made it a lot harder for me later. I thought about all the times I mentioned to her that I had a project due—I went to sleep and woke up, and the project was DONE! I know she loved me and wanted to help... I'm grown now, and I still feel like I'm catching up in certain areas and filling in gaps. I needed more structure, more boundaries. It would have helped me a lot if my parents set clear expectations for me, saying "Son, this is what we expect of you..." I realized later that it wasn't just that my older siblings were naturally self-disciplined and I wasn't, but it was that my parents prepared them differently and expected more of them. I realized that my capacity for self-discipline didn't just show up in grad school, but I could have been like that all along! If only my parents had required that of me... I could have been a straight-A student throughout high school and college!*

Remember that your teens will not articulate a desire for structure, boundaries, or responsibility because the average teenager is most interested in their concept of freedom. If you fail to be consistent disciplining each child, the consequences will become clearest in real-life scenarios when he/she needs self-discipline the most. It's up to you, the parent, to look beyond what's most comfortable for your teens now, and consistently develop in them what they'll need throughout life.

For those who have already begun spoiling your youngest,

remember that redemption is always possible. Schedule a family meeting with both parents and your youngest, letting him/her know in advance that you have something important to discuss. Then, explain the mistakes you've made in your parenting style with him/her and how you plan to adjust moving forward. Acknowledging your mistakes and articulating your intentions will prepare your teen's expectations for new standards.

One particular set of parents realized that their youngest son was becoming highly irresponsible because of their inconsistency with him. So, they decided to course-correct.

They, then, began keeping him accountable for his chores and his overall behavior. He actually did straighten up and became a responsible young man. What a great example of the power of increased consistency!

Countless examples prove that consistency is one of the most important keys to effective discipline. Parents must always keep their word concerning the consequences they promise, and they should do it *when* they say they will, which should always be soon. Why? **The consequence must be close and clearly connected to the action.**

Timing is key! Just like you want them to clean their room when you say it and not a few hours or days later, you shouldn't procrastinate either. If you wait too long after the misconduct before you discipline, the behavior won't be connected to the consequence in your teen's mind.

Teens should always know, "If I do THIS, THAT will SOON follow." Not MIGHT follow... The same mindset will guide them in the real world. "If I commit this crime or tell this lie, punishment *will* follow," not "I *might* be able to get away with it."

And definitely don't be an enabler for this kind of thinking: "It's no big deal. I'll be able to talk my way out of it like I always do." There are many situations that even the finest smooth-talkers can't get out of! So, parents, support only healthy habits in your teens.

With teens' development for their future in mind, always follow through with the consequence. Be consistent. You should not have to retract the consequence out of guilt. If it's right, follow through. **If you're emotional, don't make threats.** This idea leads us to our next discussion about making decisions based upon emotion, which also breeds inconsistency.

● ● ●

Teens should always know, "If I do THIS, THAT will SOON follow." Not MIGHT follow...

● ● ●

Principle vs. Emotion

Frustration, anger, and annoyance are natural emotions to experience with your teens, but it is inappropriate to make any of these your motivation for discipline.

Love should be the sole driving force for discipline: you love your teens enough to correct them. But, you must understand the goal of discipline. With proper perspective, discipline them based upon the lesson and not based upon your anger or frustration. **Discipline should be about them and their development and not about how you feel.**

Ask yourself, "Is this about me and my stuff or about his/her development?" If your child accidentally breaks something while running, the principle is that you told him not to run in the house because it is not safe. Therefore, you discipline. It would be an emotional decision to discipline your son because he tripped and broke the mug your deceased grandmother gave you. Now, you're so angry that you lash out: "Oh my God! You are so clumsy! Come here, it's time for a whooping!" That does not teach the child a valuable lesson, but rather allows you to release your own frustration.

Discipline does not mean, "If I'm mad, I get 'em back, but if I'm not mad, it's cool." This approach is reactive and impulsive rather than thoughtful and strategic. The reactive approach will often harm your teen versus build his/her character.

● ● ●

Love should be the sole driving force for discipline: you love your teens enough to correct them.

● ● ●

Basically, proper discipline requires maturity from the parents! Regardless of emotions, discipline should be based on principle for the teen's development and protection. It should be strategic and always executed in love.

Explaining the "Why"

"Because I said so!" is common, but counter-productive. When you're raising teens, you need them to understand *why* they are being disciplined, *why* they are advised to avoid certain environments or people, *why* they are instructed to study well...

If they don't understand why, and they are only obeying commands, they might as well be robots. You want to raise wise human beings who can think for themselves and one day be *self-disciplined*. (See "Raising Great Decision- Makers.")

Remember the goal of discipline—to develop character. In order to build character, you need to change the mindset. You should always explain why your teen is being disciplined so that he/she can understand. **Help teens understand so that they can learn.**

Dad: "Son, you're grounded. You won't be going anywhere this weekend because I told you that if you fought at school again, you would stay home over the weekend."

Teen: "What?! The whole weekend, just because I got into one fight?!"

Dad: "Yes. When you fight, you are showing everyone around you that you lack self-control. You are operating in weakness by giving others the power to anger you and make you snap. No one should have that power over you. You are stronger than that. You are a respectable young man, and respectable young men don't walk around disrespecting others through black eyes and bloody noses, no matter how much trash they talk. This weekend, you need to take a break from some of your hot-tempered friends who encourage the wrong attitude in you, and sit down to remember who you are."

Imagine how different the boy's understanding would be if the exchange went this way instead:

> *A good enough "why" will be much more productive than a "because I said so."*

Dad: "Son, you're grounded. Give me your car keys because you won't step foot out of the house this weekend."

Son: "Why? What's so bad about one fight?"

Dad: "Because I said you shouldn't fight. Go to your room."

Take the time to explain. It takes a lot more thought and energy to explain the "why" behind the "what" than to simply use the exit line, "Because I said so!" But, your teens are worth the energy that it takes to teach them, developing their judgment and character.

As kids, our mother used to tell us not to slouch, and one day, she gave us a "why" that was good enough to permanently improve our posture. While we lazily stood slouching, she said, "Alright now, you need to straighten your back before you get scoliosis. If you get scoliosis, your back will permanently have a big hump in it like 'The Hunchback of Notre Dame'. Then, you'll want to stand up straight but won't be able to. Do it now while you can." Our eyes got wide, we stiffened with fear, and we stood up straight from then forward!

Whenever we would see each other forgetfully slouch, we would say, "You better straighten your back, or you'll get scoliosis." We became one another's accountability partners so our mother didn't have to waste any more breath repeating herself. **A good enough "why" will be much more productive than a "because I said so."**

Often, teens resent their parents' discipline because they feel as if they're being punished without good reason. People respond better when they don't feel oppressed. What if they could see the situation from your perspective?

Actually, they can if you take the time to provide that understanding. Yes, some things teens won't understand until they become parents. But, there's much more that we need them to get before then so they can develop properly.

To aid understanding after your explanation, try asking your teen, "Okay, imagine for a moment that you are me and I am you. You are the parent who cares... What would you have done in this situation?"

I'm telling you, perspective changes a lot! One time our mom sat me (Kristie) down (when I was a teen) and asked me that question. It really hit home! In fact, it frustrated me that her decision made so much sense!

When I answered her question, as much as I wanted to think of a better response than the one she gave me, I couldn't. It completely changed my view of her decision. I was still mad, but I understood. Haha! And my renewed perspective yielded better decisions in my future.

Customizing the Method

When we were teenagers, the most impacting form of discipline was one of Dad's convicting lectures. These lectures meant we weren't doing it again! Our mindsets had been altered. Typically, teens decide to just "proceed with caution" after correction, but we were shook (slang for *scared*)!

Although spankings scared us growing up, lectures from Dad in our pre-teen and teenage years most developed our character. These talks helped us to truly understand the importance of making wise decisions.

You might consider us soft for this, but the lectures could make us cry just like a spanking, and they actually made us feel worse in our hearts about the misconduct. We felt more remorse, and the impact provoked very quick behavioral change and long-term character transformation. Remember that our dad is a professional communicator, so he knew what to say and how to say it in order to hit home.

Lecturing, spanking, restricting privileges, grounding,

isolation… There are many different ways to discipline, but age and personality typically determine the method you should use.

Generally, a clear and simple explanation accompanying physical correction or "time out" are all that young children can understand.

Teenagers can greatly benefit from an in-depth, tactful lecture that can be accompanied by grounding or restricting certain privileges.

Nevertheless, whatever method you choose, you must evaluate its effectiveness. Has the behavior changed? Does your teen have clear understanding?

If the behavior of your teen is worsening, it is safe to assume you should try something different.

Is the consequence actually impactful to that particular personality, or is it dreadful for one of your teens while his sibling can easily tolerate it? Sure, consistent spankings that are thoroughly explained can be effective for some people, and especially for younger children. But, pay attention if it's not working!

Instead of trying to make the spankings more and more brutal, consider trying a new method. It could be that your daughter straightens up as soon as you tell her that she can't go out with her friends for a month, while your son's behavior improves because he wants his Xbox back from you. Because each of your kids is different, take time to evaluate what works best for each person.

One of our friends received unusually cruel physical punishment growing up. She was very rebellious and stubborn, and she vocalized all of her negative attitudes. One day, her father made her take a bath, came into her bedroom while she was drying off, and spanked her while she was naked! In a different instance, he spanked her in front of her siblings, too. Needless to say, she was humiliated. Still, she remained just as rebellious.

No matter how much fear he instilled in her through his horrifying beatings, her behavior remained the same. Instead of maturing from his "correction," she felt rejected, lonely, and bitter. Clearly, her dad needed a customized method for her.

Strategic Language

Although you should never curse at your teens, this is not what this subsection is about. If your primary objective of discipline is character development, make sure you properly frame your teen's focus, using your language.

Why term it "punishment" if your objective is not to punish? You are not aiming for suffering, but again, for behavioral change and character development. Since you discipline out of love to develop responsible people, why not call it something that corresponds with your positive goals? For example, you could call it "character development."

Likewise, use positive language concerning your teens themselves. In order to do so, you must separate the action from the person. **Address negative behavior, but NEVER negatively label your teens.**

You should not call your children "bad" to their faces or to anyone else's. Yes, they will occasionally exhibit bad behavior, but so do you. Separate your teen's identity from his negative behavior so that you can build his character.

Sample 1:

> *You are an exceptional teenager, different from all the rest. What you did was not good though. You should always do the right thing because that is more becoming of who you are. Because you made a bad decision, it is time for character development. What should you have done? For the next 15 minutes, think about what you should have done differently. Then, we'll discuss what your next two weeks are gonna look like.*

Sample 2:

"Why did you lie to me? You're not a liar. You're an honest person, and I respect who you are, so please respect me enough to tell me the truth, no matter what it is. I'll have to keep your phone with me for the next few days so every time you think about using your phone, you remember how important it is to tell the truth."

The language you choose to use can damage or it can discipline. Frame your speech to maintain proper focus and accomplish the goal without forming negative identities.

● ● ●

Address negative behavior, but NEVER negatively label your teens.

● ● ●

Decisions that Last

As you discipline, remember this scripture: "Those who spare the rod of discipline hate their children. Those who love their children care enough to discipline them." —Proverbs 13:24 (NLT)

Don't let too many things "slide" because your teen is super sweet or charming, or because you don't feel like correcting. It definitely takes energy, but it has long-lasting benefits!

Let love lead you to discipline consistently, wisely, and maturely using customized methods and positive language. Your teens might never thank you; but if you discipline effectively, their lifestyles will be all the "thank you" you need.

CHAPTER 8

PURPOSEFUL PROTECTION

Sheltering Done Right

"Don't be out past midnight."

"Those are not the kinds of people you should be hanging around."

"What kind of music are you listening to?!"

...The sound of parents in protection mode!

There is a very fine line between being protective and overprotective, but it is absolutely necessary to protect your teens. **In order to raise virtuous adults, parents must shelter their teens while also preparing them for realities of the world.** This strategy is what we'll discuss in this chapter.

Now, the approach to this protection, as we will discuss later, determines whether the teen feels imprisoned or free. Believe it or not, we didn't even realize how sheltered we'd been until we were adults out of college!

Our parents obviously did a decent job with the delicate balance between being protective but not overprotective. And they clearly understood protection from various angles...

Beyond physical dangers of playing in the middle of the street and being outside after dark, there are many more threats.

Guarding the minds of your teens means that the life they do live to see is of utmost quality. We're guarding their minds and hearts so that they're in prime emotional and spiritual health in order to develop integrity.

Many teens go down the wrong paths because of exposure to the wrong people, images, situations, and doctrines. They are misguided by subtle or even blatant influences. Living in this world, it's impossible to shield your teens from everything bad, neither is that the ultimate goal. Within reason, shield them from immoral influences while also teaching them how to conduct themselves when faced with various worldviews. Being careful and realistic is key.

Sheltering Vs. Protecting

To frame our conversation, take a look at these statements from sheltered students:

> One of my guy friends mentioned "periods," and as a high school student, I asked "Are you talking about punctuation?" He said, "You don't know what a period is?! Well, I don't want to be the one to tell you that if you don't already know. Go home and ask your parents." When I asked my dad in the car one day, he got really flustered and wouldn't answer the question. So I did what any curious guy would do, and I googled it. I really wanted to know! When I googled it, I read about blood and got really grossed out. Then, I read about the word "vagina" and googled that too to find out what that was. I was shocked at the pictures that popped up on my computer screen, and I panicked! Next thing you know, I was on a Victoria's Secret webpage... All because my dad wouldn't answer my simple question... —Anonymous Male Student

"I wish my parents had explained to me how to use guns responsibly instead of just taking away all the guns that came with my toys and keeping me from watching TV or movies with gun violence." —Anonymous Student

"Until the sex education class at my college, I thought sex was two people hugging and rolling around in the bed. At the end of the semester, I told my professor, 'Thank you for teaching me what my parents never did.'" —Anonymous Student

"My parents' sheltering created a hyper-curiosity in me. It didn't protect me in the long run: it eventually made me want to experience it all for myself." —Anonymous Student

Sheltering your teens is a must; but, learning how to shelter without crippling your kids for the real world is a major challenge of parenthood.

Before moving forward, let's differentiate between our use of the word *protection* and the word *sheltering* in the context of this chapter. Yes, sheltering is a form of protection, but the term *sheltering* is used with a more specific connotation. When we say "sheltering," we're referring specifically to "shielding" your teens from exposure to particular influences that you deem negative.

You should shelter your kids for a period of time, and then loosen the reins. Allow them to experience some things in your presence and discuss the issues.

For example, when we were kids, our parents did not allow us to watch anything with profanity, sexual content, or horror elements. But during our teenage years, they allowed us to see some of these things in their presence, and then they asked us questions like, "What's wrong with this picture?"

This helped us to exercise our own judgment and process the difference between right and wrong in the media. If we weren't able to fully articulate the danger in whatever we saw on TV, they would explain it to us. This was key! We could then think for ourselves while under their protection instead of waiting until we were on our own to process those concepts.

The truth is, who's really going to go through life never hearing a curse word on TV? Not gonna happen. Like this media exposure, some things are unavoidable and should be exposed by parents who can frame them properly. The application of this concept will be discussed in more detail in the "Guarding Media" subsection of section 2 of "Purposeful Protection."

Now, let's explore an important concept: How can you nurture teens who are morally and culturally exceptional without raising socially awkward aliens?

When you raise pure-hearted leaders in your home, and you work hard to separate them from immoral influences, how can you keep them from being shocked when they encounter the pollution of the world?

In short, how can you prepare your teens for the world you're shielding them from?

For example, most protective parents strive to shield their teens from vulgar music, inappropriate TV, profanity, sexual immorality, drugs, alcohol, violence, and wild parties.

But, if you've never discussed in detail the experiences you're trying to keep them from, meaning they don't know exactly what they're missing or why, they probably won't know how to properly process what they'll one day encounter. And they'll also be curious to open Pandora's box!

Additionally, how will they respond to people who've been raised totally differently from them? One day, they'll encounter nice people who represent everything you've taught them to shun.

Think about it: We all want to raise well-rounded adults who know how to accept those who are different from them while maintaining strong personal values. Do we really want our teens to be so sheltered that they feel afraid or confused when they're around people who seem to be from a totally different world?

Simple conversations can change everything:

> *Not everyone grew up how you did. Some people didn't have the attention and resources that you've been used to, so they look for other ways to make money. This kid's only role model was a drug dealer. So, no, I don't want you involved with drugs; but, no, he's not the devil because he got caught up with the wrong people. You don't know*

what you would've done if you were in his shoes. He needs an alternative to help his family, and he needs a mentor to show him there's more to life.

Another example:

Although she's pregnant at 14 years old, you don't know how she got in this situation. She's probably been through a lot for someone so young. She might've even been raped or manipulated when she was feeling broken. Yes, premarital sex is wrong, but be careful so that you don't treat her like her identity is sin. Pray for her and always be kind. She's a human being just like you.

To avoid raising judgmental kids, these conversations should happen frequently. When living a sheltered life, it's natural to feel like an alien sometimes when you get around people whose lifestyles are extremely different from your own. And it's also natural to view the world in a very narrow-minded way, like bad people versus good ones. This can lead to judgmental attitudes towards those who are different from you.

In fact, we can remember being in college in a hotel room with two other girls who returned to the room drunk. We covered our heads with the sheets and pretended like we were asleep. We realized that we had never been that close to drunk people, and we were nervous because we didn't know what to expect. All we knew was that drunk people are unpredictable. Haha!

Also, we used to be so sheltered from profanity that when we heard a nice person use profanity, we automatically thought that they weren't as nice as we originally perceived them to be. In our minds, "Good people don't curse because cursing is wrong." The truth is that, in the real world, most people — good and bad — curse. Although cursing is not a good habit, it is also wrong to assume that someone is a complete heathen because they use a profane word.

These instances are normal for sheltered kids, but we did not feel like we were so sheltered that we could not function properly in the world. We had no problems adjusting in college, even after being homeschooled from the fifth grade through high school graduation!

How did our parents do it?

1. They had very real conversations with us often.
2. They exposed us to real-life scenarios before the world did.
3. They made sure that we knew the truth, and they framed our perspective around biblical values.

This means that, yes, we were learning about sex and its proper context when we were in elementary school, before the other kids even knew about it! We heard most major issues from our parents first, so they framed our understanding of these topics. They didn't wait for us to find out and come ask them questions, but they always stayed a step ahead and prepared us to make wise decisions.

True protection comes in practicing a healthy balance between sheltering and exposing. Parents typically focus on the sheltering part, but that alone is crippling. Many parents believe that sheltering their teens will save them from the dangers of the world. While this is true in some cases, it often does more harm than good for the development of the teen.

Often, your teens find out about everything you tried to shield them from anyway, whether through their friends at school, the Internet, or television. And then the consequences of the exposure are negative. In contrast, the exposure is beneficial when accompanied by your explanation and wisdom.

True protection comes in practicing a healthy balance between sheltering and exposing.

Since we were young, Mom was great at this balance of

exposing and sheltering. We can remember being in elementary or middle school when we were riding in our minivan, and she randomly told us what masturbation was and why it was wrong.

She said something like, "You know, many people do something that's called masturbating, which is basically having sex with yourself. Even some virgins do it and don't consider it sex. Many people don't understand that it is wrong because they say that they aren't hurting anyone. But it feeds lust, it often comes along with pornography, and it's not a good way to keep a pure mind." (Of course, she explained what pornography was as well.)

Although we still didn't understand exactly how someone has sex alone (haha), we definitely got the picture that it is wrong to satisfy your sexual desires on yourself in whatever way. Her conversation with us was very impactful because she managed to be the *first* one to tell us about masturbation. We never forgot this minivan discussion that exposed us to this topic from a Christian perspective.

Instead of providing wisdom and preparation, certain expressions of sheltering leave children naive. Teens end up more susceptible to become prey of all that you attempted to shield them from. The truth is, they'll find out at some point from someone, and it might as well be you! That way, you can shape their views according to your family's values.

In other cases, sheltering yields poor judgment in teens because they weren't allowed to practice making decisions under your supervision. They also might be resentful towards you for robbing them of freedom to make their own choices. Finally, they just might rebel anyway, and then your relationship with them becomes strained.

One student said that her mom forbid her to date. She later admitted that she wished her mother had helped her to understand why she shouldn't date versus commanding her not to do so.

● ● ●

*Remember, wisely balance exposure + sheltering to = **protection.***

● ● ●

Without her mother's knowledge, she began dating when she was fourteen years old. Her mother had not discussed the importance of abstinence, the relevance of maturity level in relationships, or any dating advice for that matter. Mom simply said she was too young.

Because this teen was so sheltered and uneducated about dating, she was more vulnerable to deception by guys, which led her to poor decision-making. She said that she didn't feel comfortable talking to her mom about anything once she got into a relationship, but her boyfriend exposed her to quite a lot. She explained how hiding became a way of life for her. She was very naive and was, by default, taught by her peers instead of by her mother.

In her first romantic relationship, which lasted four years, she was abused verbally and physically. Her young boyfriend even choked her AFTER she had given him her virginity. Still, she sought no guidance from her mother who had no clue that her forbidden boyfriend existed.

She felt that every time she made a mistake, her mom would either fuss, yell, or nag—so why bother?

Her mom obviously loved her dearly. She set parameters in order to keep her daughter safe. She was concerned about her well-being. Nevertheless, she used an ineffective strategy.

Instead of informing her, she sheltered her. Instead of empowering her with understanding, she made the decisions for her. Instead of welcoming her daughter's feedback, she intimidated her. Instead of making herself approachable, she repelled her daughter by harsh reactions.

Her sweet, prized, and beautiful daughter ended up deceived, abused, insecure, and distrusting. Her mother couldn't sufficiently protect her because she was denied access into her daughter's personal life. This access is what we pray you will gain (See "Friend or Parent" for details.).

Furthermore, her protection strategy was ineffective because she sheltered her daughter without adequately informing her. Remember, wisely balance **exposure** + **sheltering** to = *protection*.

What to Look out for

Beyond sheltering, let's discuss just a few of the vitally important elements that parents should consider in the practice of purposeful protection.

Helpful or Harmful Friendships

The Bible says, "Bad company ruins good morals," and it is true that even the most well-mannered teens get into trouble by association with the wrong types of friends. Not only does their behavior change, but also, their mindsets become corrupted. Parents should always know who their teens are spending their time with.

Whenever we asked to go out with friends, "Who's going?" was our parents' first question. They did not forbid us from going out with certain people, but we knew when they were making excuses about why we should stay home that day... It was really because of who was going.

That always made the difference. To some, they responded enthusiastically and, to others, very hesitantly.

A classic excuse from Dad—"You girls will be too tired to go because you would've already had a long day, and then you'll have a super early morning the very next day." They always made it clear to us verbally and nonverbally who they thought was good company and who was not.

For some reason, our parents always knew from the very beginning of each relationship whether the friendship would be productive or harmful to us. Our mom would say, "She's not who you think she is." We would wonder, "How do you know this?" And we would soon discover that her seemingly premature analysis was undeniably accurate.

One particular girl began pursuing our friendship not long before our mother basically said "She's not your kind." We could not understand why Mom felt so strongly, even though she had not engaged in one conversation with the girl.

Within weeks, the girl asked my (Kirstie's) boyfriend to go on a vacation with her and some of her friends without even inviting ME! (He didn't go with her, of course.) When I texted her to find out why she did that, she cursed me out instead of apologizing.

Immediately, we knew our mom was right, and we never spoke to her again.

It is clear that parents should communicate their disapproval of unhealthy associations, but how those sentiments are expressed is also noteworthy. Parents, be careful not to verbally attack the individual because then your teens become defensive. In defense mode, they'll ignore you and won't receive even your constructive feedback.

We can recall one particular instance when our parents made that mistake. We perceived their language as a brutal attack of our closest friend. The discussion ended with both of us in anger and tears. "You don't even know him!" we said. Not only did we not believe what they said, but also we ignored their advice.

We all look back on that instance now and laugh, our parents making fun of us for our tears and defensiveness, since they were soon proven right. We can laugh with them now, but we were not listening then.

We didn't listen until our dad came to our room weeks later, sat on one of our twin beds, and calmly explained to us what God revealed to him concerning the detriment of this friendship. We were deeply disturbed. We immediately decided to make the hard choice to let go of our best friend.

After we distanced ourselves from him, we were able to see how we had already changed negatively during the friendship. We were shocked and disappointed that we hadn't noticed it sooner. We actually thought we were helping him (which we were), but at the same time, we were becoming more like him.

Parents, remain calm while speaking honestly, saying what is necessary for understanding, while avoiding the appearance of bashing. Make sure you point out the positive qualities of your teen's friend in addition to the alarming ones. Remember, in your teen's mind, the friend is ALL good, while in your mind, he/she is poison. Haha! Acknowledge both sides in order to paint a more realistic picture for your teen that is easier to accept.

Here's an example:

> Honey, I know Zach is always there when you need him, and he's a lot of fun. He keeps you laughing. He's good at that, and I can see why he's your best friend. But, please hear me when I say that Zach is not a good influence on you. When you're around him, you act more careless and reckless. And because he's disrespectful to his parents, your mom and I have noticed you being disrespectful to us more often. Zach is not concerned about going to college or investing in his future in other ways. Birds of a feather not only flock together, but they also fly to the same destination. He will rub off on you more than you think if you stay close to him. We love you... Please be wise about this. We know you have it in you to make hard choices that will produce long-term success.

Your teens will probably become defensive either way, but one approach stirs anger and the other welcomes a calm discussion.

Your warning probably won't see immediate results, but it will linger in their minds and cause them to evaluate the person a little more carefully. The hope is that they agree with you or trust your word enough that they begin to distance themselves from that harmful relationship. But sometimes it takes time.

If something that you said starts to prove the slightest bit true, your teen more quickly notices it and likely proceeds with greater caution. The more instances your word is proven true, the more likely it becomes that your teen will trust you next time.

Your teens' friends can lead them into many dangers and

immorality you would want to protect them from (e.g. rebellion, lying, pornography, drugs, alcohol, premarital sex, academic failure), or they can reinforce the values you've instilled because they live with integrity also.

Since you have much more experience, and therefore, your discernment should be keener, help your teens select friends. You can shield them from destructive influences and help them select loyal friends who share their values. The right friends will encourage your teens to be their best and provide vital support for their journey.

Guarding Media

Other influences in your teens' lives that need filters are music, television shows, and movies that glamorize what you've warned them against. These songs and images repeat in their minds, teaching them the opposite of what you value.

Use media as discussion pieces about real life consequences for the particular choices displayed. Discuss whether or not the consequences are realistically or unrealistically portrayed in the music, movie, or TV show.

Here's an example:

[While a song is playing in the department store]

What do you think about what he's saying in this song? Are money, cars, and clothes enough to make people happy? Is it okay to sabotage others in order to "make it to the top"? What does it mean to be truly successful? How can greed actually destroy lives and relationships?

Here's another example:

[While watching a movie]

What did y'all think about his choice? So he's not "in love with" his wife anymore and starts having sex with her best friend... Of course he's feeling good with her! That's how he was with his wife at the beginning too, and then they became busy and stressed through life, focusing on the negative aspects instead of the positives of each other. In real life, with his mentality, do you think he could marry the best friend and be happy with her forever, never getting bored? How do you think he damaged his wife, his kids, his finances, and himself through his decisions? How do you think this movie portrayed marriage to be in comparison to an affair? Is it realistic to make healthy, life-altering choices when driven by lust and emotions?

● ● ●

Excess privacy is a powerful tool for risky behavior.

● ● ●

As the examples above illustrate, **use strategic questions to help your teens understand and process concepts in the media.** Teach them in a practical way why they shouldn't watch or listen to certain things. And make sure you clearly establish the standard of what is acceptable and what is not. With an enlightened perspective, they'll be more equipped to make better choices in media and in life.

A specific element of media that is highly addictive and destructive for the young and old alike is pornography. Parents should purchase computer and phone software that will block pornography sources because addiction is fast and easy. Try K9 for computers, Ever Accountable for Androids, and Spyware for iPhones.

Another helpful tip is this: Establish a household policy where all doors must remain unlocked inside the house. Not only are locked doors hazardous in case of a fire, but **excess privacy is a powerful tool for risky behavior.** Increase the risk of getting caught and simultaneously decrease the opportunity for risky behavior.

Scary enough, it has been scientifically proven that pornography shrinks a part of the brain because of the brain's plasticity.

The brain was designed to change based on what it's repeatedly exposed to. It's adaptable.

Unfortunately, pornography not only fills people with lust, wastes valuable time (numerous hours in addiction), and creates an obsession with sexuality, but this addiction to pixels on a screen is also proven to disturb the health of relationships.

A countless number of marriages are destroyed because one person cannot properly perform sexually without watching a pornographic image. It can also lead to infidelity.

Crazy enough, one guy reported that, on his wedding day, he was so full of lust that he found himself undressing the bridesmaids in his mind. And on his honeymoon, he was mentally having sex with the hotel employees. He didn't even have sex with his wife on their wedding night because he was so addicted to "pixels" that his real life wife didn't arouse him enough.

His addiction eventually led him to an affair with a female sex addict who, in some way, fulfilled his pornographic fantasies. He described her as being "porn with skin on." In total, he was addicted to pornography for twenty years before he found freedom.

Addictions this strong often begin as young as middle school and high school. Many report exposure in elementary school. Protecting your kids from pornography does not mean ensuring that their eyes never see any form of porn. In today's society, that's impossible. Porn is more accessible (Internet) and affordable (sometimes FREE) than it's ever been in history, and the sex industry is making billions of dollars from destroying people's lives through this addiction.

For those with young kids, it is 100% necessary to talk to them about what pornography is and why it's so dangerous. Be the first to explain it to them so that you can frame it properly.

Don't let another child at school show your kids porn on a cell phone, peaking their curiosity before *you've* warned them. By the time they stumble upon porn one day, they should already know *from you* exactly why they should turn their heads and close their eyes immediately, before they become addicted.

We were first exposed to pornography in elementary school by the neighbor's kids who were our same age. (Remember that we were homeschooled PKs, so if it can happen to us, it can happen to anyone!) Fortunately for us, our parents randomly decided to talk to us about pornography before we had the chance to get hooked. They had no idea what our neighbors had shown us, yet they gave us a timely speech exposing the dangers of porn.

Take a look at the thoughts of this young adult who got addicted to pornography at a young age:

> *I wish my dad had talked to me about porn and sex like my mom talked to my sisters. He never talked to me about sex. I definitely plan to talk to my sons about it because I feel like it would have changed a lot for me. Mom tried to talk to me about it here and there, but it was too awkward and uncomfortable coming from her. I needed to hear it from Dad. I'm gonna be vulnerable with my kids about my mistakes and help them avoid the same things.*

Because sexual matters are uncomfortable topics for many parents, it is preferable for men to talk to boys and women to girls, when possible. Whether that's a parent or a mentor, these conversations are a must.

Don't let your kids bump into porn in ignorance. Sheltering them from the term *pornography* won't help. This kind of ignorance is not "bliss," but it is dangerous. You can start by saying "naked people" because you should talk to them so early that *pornography* is too long of a word for them to handle. But do teach them. Expose them tactfully with your words and empower them to do the right thing before they ever see porn with their own eyes. If you have teens that are already exposed, it's time now to have a real conversation.

Protecting Faith

If you're a spiritual parent and you want to guard your teens against false doctrines, you must be intentional. Protecting your child's faith does not happen by accident.

Our family is unashamedly Christian, loving Jesus Christ with all of our hearts. We believe that the entire Bible is the true, inspired Word of God. Clearly, much of today's society opposes many biblical principles.

This is why Christian parents have to bring awareness to the difference between societal values and biblical truths. The latter is quite counter-cultural!

For example, most people love only those who love them and seek revenge when someone hurts them. In contrast, the Bible teaches us to love even our enemies! Love when it's hard, pray for those who use you, and give to those who can't pay you back. Let God deal with those who mistreat you. God says that the world will know we are His by the way we love each other.

Another difference is that American society says that, if you're an adult or if you're in love, sex outside of marriage is acceptable. These days, people often condone promiscuity, as long as the individual uses "protection" and is a "responsible adult."

We believe that sex is wrong when the two people are not married to each other because the Bible calls that "fornication," which is a sin. When you consider all the drama, STDs, broken hearts, fatherlessness, and dangerous situations that arise because of sex outside of marriage, you can deduce that Father God is trying to protect us.

As we protect our teens, we must use the Bible as the filter for the faithlessness of our environment. Consider the theory of evolution which contradicts the Bible, yet permeates the education system now.

Many young Christians in America now are confused about whether or not evolution is true. And therefore, they're questioning the verity of the Bible. "Did God really create everything, or did all of this just sprout out of nothing? At school, everyone is telling me that creation, as I learned in Sunday school, is a fairy tale."

Undoubtedly, it's necessary to teach your kids biblically based truth. The Bible has taught us scientific facts before scientists even discovered them! For example, scientists thought that the earth was flat while the Bible already taught that it's round.

Science has to catch up to the Bible because the Bible *is* scientific, in its truest form. *Real* science and the Bible do not contradict, but go hand-in-hand. Teach your kids what's proven true versus what's still just scientific "theory."

Our parents had many in-depth conversations with us at young ages about the truth of the Bible versus the standards that our society embraces. Without those conversations, we probably wouldn't have married as virgins or known what to believe about many important topics as teens.

Although all Christians must study the Bible for themselves, the Bible is so long and extensive that it could take many more years for teens to learn important values if they solely depend on their personal biblical studies. Even church attendance alone doesn't always guarantee the foundational teaching that young Christians need.

When we went to college, we heard many professors attacking tenets of the Bible and supposedly discrediting several teachings we knew to be true. In addition to our own biblical studies, the teaching from our parents helped us remain firm in our faith, even in challenging times.

To adequately protect your teen's faith, you don't have to preach sermons at home everyday. Simply initiate meaningful dialogue every time you see an opportunity.

For instance, your teen will come home from school some days telling you something a classmate said that should prompt productive conversation.

Here are a few common examples:

"Only people like murderers go to Hell. You don't really

have to believe that Jesus is the only way to Heaven. God is love, so He doesn't send a lot of people to Hell." Or "If God is so good, why does He let bad things happen to good people?" Or "Oral sex isn't wrong because it's not even sex."

Just talk. If you need to look it up in the Bible yourself (e.g. via Google) to find out the truth or a practical way to explain it, do that. Don't be embarrassed to tell your teens, "Hold on, I'm not quite sure about that one. Let me look it up." Do your best to establish a firm foundation for them to stand on.

Balance of Protection

"How can we adequately protect without suffocating our teens?" you might ask.

Focus more on what is permissible than what is off-limits. Refrain from repeatedly emphasizing the restrictions and what they're "forbidden" to do. Use subtle methods to guide them away from certain people or things without blatantly fussing about why not and seeming to say "no" all the time.

Notice how the following example subtly avoids the situation without verbally forbidding and blatantly saying "no." Teen girl: "Hey Dad! Can I go out with Bobby, Stacie, and Rudy to the movies on Saturday?" Dad: "We would like you to stay home on Saturday night so the family can watch a movie together." Or "Have you finished your homework? What about your chores for the week?"

She can't say Dad forbid her, but over time, she understands that her father doesn't like for her to hang out with those people. It's not harsh, but it's subtle and effective redirection.

Now, to be clear, our parents did tactfully verbalize what they thought were unhealthy relationships for us, but they typically did not forbid us to keep those relationships. They also didn't bring it up EVERY time we asked to go out with those individuals. But they found ways to limit the time we spent with them.

Additionally, ask your teens questions to help them analyze situations and put them in your shoes. That way, they better understand your decision-making process. "If you had a son who wanted to attend a house party in a high-crime neighborhood at night without parental supervision, would you let him? What are some of the potential dangers in a scenario like this? If you were me, what would you do?" Help them to come to the same conclusions that you have, and make it completely clear to them why you make your decisions.

Also, constantly reiterate that your guidance is driven by love. The hope is that they don't feel like you're saying "no" for fun or even for punishment, but from a good place. **The more your teens understand your decisions and your motives, the less they will resent you.**

Furthermore, regularly affirm your teens, telling them that they are special, different from everyone else, mature, wise, and destined for greatness. Help them to understand the strength and beauty of their purity so that they're not embarrassed or ashamed of it.

And teach them the leadership that is required when you stand alone, making wise choices when others don't. Leadership sometimes feels lonely. But conformity is for cowards! Help them understand that leadership is for the strong, while conformity is for the weak. The sooner they embrace and pursue this leadership, the better decisions they'll make.

Because our parents didn't seem to say "no" all the time or constantly forbid us from everything, we felt even more free than our peers who weren't pastor's kids! We didn't realize until pretty recently how we didn't go to many sleepovers when we were young, and we weren't at many parties. We did, however, host many sleepovers at our house (under our parents' supervision), go to the mall and movies a lot, and had plenty of fun within their boundaries.

We realized which friends they

> *The more your teens understand your decisions and your motives, the less they will resent you.*

liked and didn't like through their excuses (haha!) and candid conversations, but we didn't feel robbed of our freedom to choose.

As a result, we didn't rebel or feel a strong desire to do so. To the contrary, we obeyed their counsel and boundaries, besides a few sneaky moments. Because we were very well protected, but didn't feel suffocated, we never tried to devise our escape plan.

Your Choice

Protecting your teens requires energy, meaningful conversations, and wisdom. When they're teenagers, it's not as simple as making sure they don't touch a hot stove or fall off a bike. Protection is needed in much deeper matters of the heart, mind, and spirit.

Protect them, even when that means you're thinking through more details every day than the average parent, and even when your teens have a hard time understanding your choices. Take the time to teach them what choices to make and why. From your wisdom and love, protect your teens using a foundation of truth that will equip them for moral success.

CHAPTER 9
RAISING GREAT DECISION-MAKERS

The Foundation

"Leader?! I'm not a leader!" We can so clearly recall when we thought we were incapable of leadership. Well, look at us now... We have led numerous people in different realms of influence, and we train other leaders! Want to know where it started? A day we will never forget in the living room at home...

This story is proof that sometimes parents have to take a risk in order to teach a lasting lesson, one that is unforgettable.

"Dad couldn't possibly be okay with this... (nervous gulp) What is he thinking right now?"

To get to know our new neighbors that were around our age, we and our siblings invited them to our house for a movie. They brought the movie, and it was definitely not one for 11-13 year olds.

We squirmed in our seats on the sofa as we glanced back and forth between the TV screen and our father's face. Why? Because he sat in the room the entire time, watching the movie with us.

As we were being exposed to excessive profanity, occasional nudity, and vulgar jokes, we wondered if Dad was going to interject, and we repeatedly contemplated getting up to stop the film ourselves. Nevertheless, neither happened. We sat frozen, and Dad remained calm.

We were so confused. "What is happening right now?!" we mentally exclaimed. "The most inappropriate movie we've ever seen is playing in Bishop Bronner's living room in front of a small group of teens and pre-teens, and he is only laughing! We know him, and we know that he's not okay with this! Is he cool with this? Are we just thinking too hard about it?" We wanted to know what was really going on. Well, we soon found out...

As soon as the movie ended, the neighbors went home, and we were all left in an awkward silence. Before we could go upstairs to our rooms, we discovered why Dad was so quiet. This was one of the most convicting lectures we'd ever received.

The entire duration of the movie, Dad was giving us the opportunity to be responsible and handle the situation appropriately. If you haven't caught it by now, we failed!

He taught us that day that "Silence shows consent." And he emphasized the importance of rising up as leaders instead of waiting for someone else to take the lead. He told us that he was not going to do it for us.

Dad made it clear that he was disappointed in us. He gave us the opportunity to exercise our leadership without his interference, and we didn't take it. Too timid to overcome the peer pressure, we did not stand up for what we knew was right.

Dad didn't yell, but his serious tone communicated the gravity of our mistake. The weight of his lecture sank deep into our hearts, and we respected every word.

After returning to our room, we cried our eyeballs out! We felt so bad that we had allowed fear to stop us from doing the right thing. We also felt a little anger, embarrassment, and even incompetence.

Fortunately, that feeling was disturbing enough that we

knew we never wanted to feel it again. Although we had previously thought we were incapable of being leaders because of our shyness, we became leaders after that day.

Doing what's right, no matter how you feel or what people might think—that's leadership, and that's how we learned to operate. This was the beginning of our leadership among our peers. Even though we knew we could not

● ● ●

Don't raise teens who only do well when you're around: develop thinkers who are wise enough to discern right from wrong and courageous enough to follow through.

● ● ●

immediately eliminate our shyness, we then understood that we could be leaders in spite of it.

If you don't teach your teens what leadership is, show them how to lead, and then give them the opportunity to lead, you will raise followers and not leaders. If they are followers, they will automatically imitate the poor decisions of their friends.

Don't raise teens who only do well when you're around: develop thinkers who are wise enough to discern right from wrong and courageous enough to follow through.

Let's talk about how you can do your part in turning "average" teenagers into leaders—how you can raise great decision-makers.

Parents' Part

"What an idiot! Why, after all this time that you've been so responsible would you go to college playing around and lose your scholarship?!"

"Why would you watch your older sister get pregnant out of wedlock, suffering through depression, and then go have unprotected sex and do the same thing?"

"What would make you try drugs with some troublemakers when you already see where their lives are headed?!"

Have you ever wondered why teens make such stupid choices sometimes? Have you questioned whether or not they have common sense or any kind of moral filter?

Well, not all bad decisions are avoidable, but we want to discuss what parents *can* do to raise great decision-makers.

If you expect your teens to make the right decisions, you'll have to teach them how to do so. The truth is, there is no such thing as common sense: sense is not common!

Too often, parents expect their teens to automatically know things because it sounds simple. Just like you intentionally teach your kids how to ride a bike or pick up any other behavior that you hope becomes second-nature for them, you should teach them how to make good choices.

Explain what the right decisions are, *why* those decisions are correct, and then take the training wheels off. Remove your hands, and let them practice while they're still within your oversight.

"Don't watch those kinds of movies"—Not a good idea. Better—"Don't watch those kinds of movies because the images will replay in your mind over and over. And eventually you might find yourself with fears you wish you could erase!"

Notice that an easy "Because I said so" is not beneficial for the decision-making ability of your teen. So work a little harder to be clear.

"Don't hang out with people like that!" Not just "because I said so," but instead, try this:

> ...Because people like that are so nice, but they slowly turn you into someone you don't want to be. When I was in high school, one of my best friends was just like your friend, Eric. When I was around him, I felt like I had a real friend. He always had my back. But at the same time, he pulled out the devious side of me. I started sneaking around behind my parents' backs more than ever. Hiding things from them became the new norm. I realized I was becoming someone else... Because I wanted him to think I

was cool, I did a lot of things I regret. Some things, you
can never take back, no matter how much you want to…

Use conversations like this to give your teens a glimpse of your adult brain so they can understand how it operates and why. Then, they can discover the value of making those kinds of decisions.

Many parents foster mental weakness in their teens that sometimes isn't fully revealed until the teen has left home.

Think of it like this: You never want to keep the training wheels on so long that your kids never really learn how to ride a bike with you. One day in college, the military, or in the workforce, LIFE will snatch off those training wheels. If they've never practiced with your assistance, they are much more likely to fall when it counts.

Brian: "I can't hang out with you anymore."

The "Bad" Friend: "Why not?"

Brian: "I don't know, man. Because my dad said I can't."

When Brian gets to college, this same ignorance will lead him to entertain the wrong friends when his father isn't there to dictate who he can and cannot be friends with. He never learned the art of making wise decisions for himself, given the necessary information.

Don't raise dependents: Raise decision-makers.

Teaching your teens how to make good decisions matures them. And it gives them more confidence in their own moral character versus just dependence upon yours. It also provides clarity that can avoid some resentment, therefore cultivating a healthier parent-teen relationship. Furthermore, it demonstrates to them that you trust them and believe in their potential.

If you ever wonder why teens make better decisions while they're living at home than when they move out, here's a little food for thought: Maybe it's because it was never the teens making those "right" choices at home. Maybe that was the result of parental control. Then, when mom and dad are no longer around, teens finally have the freedom to make their own decisions. By this point, though, they only have the guidance of their friends.

Be intentional to train your teens in the art of good decision-making. Yes, they are ultimately responsible for their own choices, but their success starts with you.

BE It

> I really did do the paper, Ms. Walton. I did the whole thing! And then while I was doing my community service at the nursing home, as I often like to do in my free time, a gangster ran in! Ms. Betty's grandson, who was there visiting her, had lost his cocaine. Anyway, as I was drying off Ms. Betty's dentures, shots were fired, and my completed paper, which was on the coffee table, was splattered with blood. I know I could've brought it as proof, but I believe in honoring the dead, and flaunting their blood is not the way to do that. So I laid it in the coffin with Ms. Betty's grandson. My computer happened to have crashed, so there is no trace of my paper. I spent my evening comforting Ms. Betty and giving her a massage to ease her pain. So, you see, Ms. Walton, unlucky circumstances made me late on my paper. May I have an extension please?

Immediately following his passionate plea, he passes the phone to his teacher with his mom on the other end. She, then, verifies his story so the teacher won't fail him.

This situation is wrong in so many ways. First of all, his story was completely fabricated, which you've probably noticed. Second of all, his mother validated his lie. In instances like these, even if it would cause your teen to flunk and retake a class, you must enforce the right thing.

It is even the little things that directly or indirectly teach your kids how to think. When you allow the end result to justify your immoral route to the goal, you authorize your teens to do the same, compromising their integrity.

If you want your teens to make wise decisions, you must enforce proper values. Our father teaches that when you make your decisions based upon principle, 99% of your decisions are already made.

If your teens don't have the right values, they will act according to what they "feel" at the moment, which will lead them in a million different directions that usually won't end well.

The Bible says, "Train up a child in the way he should go: and when he is old, he will not depart from it"—Proverbs 22:6 KJV. Therefore, you first have to train your children. Intentionally instill the values in your teens that you want them to carry with them for the rest of their lives. In order to raise great decision-makers, you should heed the following process:

1. Establish your family's values.
2. Determine how you will develop their decision-making abilities.
3. Examine how you model the values they should embody.

A friend was very inspiring, as he explained how he intentionally instilled certain values in his kids. For instance, he wanted to teach his children to be producers and not just consumers.

He told them the value repeatedly; he was a creator of many things himself, including websites, videos, and paintings; and he used a timer app called "Moments" to monitor his phone and iPad usage. Accordingly, he taught his children how to make and edit videos, create artwork, play on technology in moderation, and use creativity. At elementary school ages, his kids were extremely intelligent, creative, and exceptional producers of projects.

If you don't actually model what you teach your teens to be, your teachings are in vain.

Your actions will either strengthen or deplete the value of your words.

Your actions truly do speak louder than your words. And **your actions will either strengthen or deplete the value of your words.**

"You teach what you know, but you reproduce who you are." —Bishop Dale C. Bronner

Perfect example: Many people assume that we were forced to volunteer at our father's church, teach Sunday school, sing in the choir, and lead worship. Some assume that our parents pressured all of their kids to work for the church in adulthood. The truth is, we saw our parents model church involvement past the call of duty. They loved helping others through full-time ministry; and eventually, we discovered why. We followed in their footsteps! They actually did reproduce themselves in incredibly obvious and meaningful ways.

What if you feel like you've already demonstrated the wrong habits to your teens? It is not too late to change and become the role model that you want to be.

In fact, tell your teens that you've decided to change, and explain to them what you plan to do differently. That way, they know what to expect and don't feel as tempted to consider you a hypocrite when you give them advice that contradicts your past behavior.

Acknowledge your past behavior, clarify your future choices, and move on. In doing this, you also model determination, repentance, and humility. You show them that it is never too late to become who you want to be.

The main reason we adopted the values of our parents is that they actually lived them. For example, we adopted their value of abstinence. They practiced abstinence from sex before marriage; taught us to do the same and explained why; and gave us strategy to avoid sexual immorality. Consequently, we remained virgins until marriage.

Now, this was not a one-time discussion, but our parents reiterated this value consistently. Our mom repeatedly discussed abstinence from elementary school to college. And our father took each of us to purchase a covenant ring; scheduled a nice dinner; discussed with us the meaning of making this promise to ourselves and to God; and guided us into sealing the deal. He helped us to understand the value of this occasion, and we were actually very excited about it!

Our parents' examples, passionate teachings, and regular accountability made such a strong impression upon us from a young age that we told ourselves that sex before marriage was not an option.

Additionally, we have never heard profanity come from our parents' mouths, and we don't use it either. Our father taught us that we should have a vocabulary extensive enough to express ourselves more intelligently.

To be honest, though, their example alone formed our learned language. Notice how the language people learn at home is always their first language, no matter what country they live in.

There was, however, a word that our mom told us to never say. We will leave this word unsaid to save her the embarrassment. Haha! This was not profanity, but not a good word either.

We cracked up laughing when she said it out of anger every now and then. As children, we told her that since she said it, we would say it too. She quickly said, "No! Don't do that!"

Nevertheless, we have definitely used that word at times, and we aren't strongly convicted that we shouldn't. Why? Because Mom *said* not to say it, but her actions spoke much louder than her words did. Fortunately, most of the words we caught were good ones. Haha!

Because of Mom and Dad, our language was more than just "profanity-free," but it was also full of blessings. They taught us to speak life! In other words, speak positively. Use words that are uplifting, encouraging, and optimistic. Our father used to say that he was allergic to negativity, and his language was surely proof of that!

Even when our parents weren't feeling well, they would

never say, "I'm sick." But they would always say, "I'm catching a healing!" Consequently, people laugh at us when we say that, too. Haha! Sounds a little weird, but it sure is positive framing.

Our parents also transferred the value of maintaining a great attitude. We would hear them rave over someone's exceptional attitude, even if it was a stranger.

Our dad would say, "Even if a person doesn't have much skill, they at least need to have a positive attitude! You can train people to be more skilled, but you should hire people with great attitudes."

Another comment Dad used to frame our attitude was this: "If you look for something negative, you can always find it. [So choose to focus on the positive.]"

Our mom taught us to always look on the bright side, "put on our rose-colored glasses," and count our blessings. She would say, "If you look at life through dark shades, the sky will appear dark and dreary to you. But if you put on your rose-colored glasses, the world will look rosy to you. It is not what you are looking at, but it is how you are looking at it."

As you can see, our parents cultivated a positive atmosphere in our home so that it was a place of peace, a place we enjoyed living. It was no accident that we were never itching and squirming to move away from home as soon as we got the chance.

They modeled positivity, and they reaped a lot more positivity than most parents get from their teens.

Practicing what you preach is more than half the battle...

In addition to positivity, our parents taught us that honesty is not always easy, but it is ultimately rewarded. Of course, we believed the "mommy myths" about our tears running out if we kept crying, but our parents didn't lie to us out of their convenience or because they thought we couldn't handle the truth. Not only were they always honest with us, but also, we observed their being honest with others.

They never even asked us to lie for them so they could dodge a dreaded phone call!

Although many accept lying as a typical teenage phase, our parents set a different standard, and we rose to the occasion. We never heard them lie, and the moral bar remained high for us.

We cannot emphasize enough that parents must model proper values for their teens or their words are meaningless. **And if a teen's values are misplaced, so will his decisions be.** If you want to raise great decision-makers, make good decisions and firmly establish values to govern the decisions of your household.

The Strategy

Strategically Developing Thinkers

Parent: "What would you do if you were out on a date with a boy and he refused to let you out of his car later in the night? He locked the doors, put his hand on your upper thigh, and tried to kiss you…"

Daughter: "That would not happen!"

Parent: "It might, but even if not, let's pretend…"

Daughter: "Okay, well, I'd just pull out some pepper spray and shoot him straight in the eyes!"

Parent: "That's good and all, but you don't even own any pepper spray. This might be a good reminder to buy some, but since you don't currently have any, what else could you do?"

Daughter: "I would tell him to get off of me and take me home. If he still kept going, I would punch him in his nuts, and jump out of the car. Then I would call you to come pick me up."

Parents, what if you purposefully sharpened your teens' decision-making skills by prompting them to exercise these abilities? We received this kind of training in our home, which prepared us to think through scenarios that most teenagers don't.

As a parent, you can create these kinds of scenarios in regular conversation during dinner time, in the car, or at home. Train them through hypothetical scenarios to make the right choices before the situation even presents itself.

Not all of the scenarios have to be emergency situations, however. You can help them think through situations with certain types of friends, teachers, or even problems they might encounter with employers.

For instance, you could ask, "What would you do if your friend offered you money that you know he stole from the register at his job?"

These kinds of questions helped us to evaluate our relationships, our desires, and what we should and should not allow before the situation presented itself.

We certainly did encounter some of the situations our parents presented to us, and because we had already processed them, we were better equipped to make the right decisions in the moment.

Other helpful scenarios could include moments of extreme anger. How would your teens respond? How *should* they respond? You certainly don't want their impulses to result in your bailing them out of jail!

Another way to strategically develop "thinkers" in your home is to talk your teens through proper ways to process some of the things they see. For instance, while watching a movie, parents could comment on the scenario, like the following:

> *Oh wow... Did you see how that guy just kept lying to cover his tracks at school, at work, with his family...? Do you really think he would've gotten away with all that in real life, especially when he started mixing the lies?! What do you think really would've happened when his boss connected the dots and found out about the money he stole? Would it really have been worth it to destroy trust in his relationships, lose his job, go to jail, and even hate himself after all his selfish acts?*

Our parents made a practice of using television to help us understand the consequences of choices.

Another interesting thing our father helped us to process was customer service. He further developed our thinking skills by highlighting small things that the average person wouldn't notice.

We were trained to notice the difference between good customer service, mediocre customer service, and bad customer service. And in the process, we learned how to provide quality customer service to others.

When we went to restaurants, our father would often offer critiques like this after the server walked away:

"See, a good server would come closer to the customer to take his order instead of expecting the customer to shout across

● ● ●

You have to give your teens the opportunity to lead, even if it means they fail in the moment.

● ● ●

the table. This server should be smiling more. I love when people serve like they love what they do!"

"If I were the owner, I would teach my employees how to serve with excellence! They've got to move faster and be pleasant even when having a bad day! Don't bring your personal life onto the job."

We learned how to serve with excellence long before we needed those skills. Our father made detailed comments on a regular basis that taught us a lot, and he continues to do the same. It was no wonder that we served so fabulously at McDonald's (our first job), at Bronner Brothers hair care company, and later at the church!

The treasure in this practice is that we didn't just hear our father complaining, but we discussed solutions to problems together. Consequently, we learned how to excel in various ways. Isn't it something how little habits like strategic conversations can make such a big impact on your teens?!

Developing Leadership

Recall the story in section 1 about how our dad remained silent during the vulgar movie and then reprimanded us for missing our opportunity to stand for what's right.

It was a painful, unforgettable lesson that impacted our leadership forever.

You have to learn when to step out of the way so that your teens can practice leading within the safety of your presence. Sometimes, that practice will be uncomfortable for you, just as the scenario with our father and the movie. Undoubtedly, he was cringing inside.

However, **you have to give your teens the opportunity to lead, even if it means they fail in the moment.**

Our mother also practiced stepping aside and thrusting us into leadership, in a different way. Although worship through song is also her passion, she valued developing her teens so that we could learn to lead as well.

She used to sing the lead part with the youth ensemble (worship team), ad-libbing and directing the order of song to the band and the singers. We felt comfortable singing in the background and were perfectly happy to stay there.

"You two know that you are fully capable of leading," she would say. "Pretty soon, I am not going to come up here with you." We kept assuring her that we did not want to lead, and that we were comfortable where we were, following her.

One service, she finally didn't sing with us. That night, we discovered that we actually could lead the songs, ad-libbing and indicating the order of song.

She then pushed us to start greeting the congregation before worship. This terrified us! That would cause us to be the first voice on the microphone, charged with filling the room with energy and encouraging everyone to get up and participate.

She still said, "You two are well able to do a great job at it!" Again, she refused to do it for us, leaving us with no choice but to embrace the responsibility.

To our surprise, she had trained us well, and we did not fail.

Because she first taught us what to do, showed us how to do it, and then gave us the freedom to lead while in her presence, we became strong leaders that she could trust in her absence.

Not only in leading worship did she allow us to take the lead, but also in the ministries, special events, and programs we later developed. She assisted us when we needed her, but she refused to cripple us.

Sometimes we asked her what decision she thought we should make, and she would either give her input or she would say, "This is your baby. You do what you have in your heart to do, and that will be fine with me."

Some might have found our parents' approach a little hard to fathom, thinking, "Well, you're the mom… you're the dad… Why don't you do what parents do and control the situation?! You should be telling *them* what to do!"

But they did exactly what parents should do. They trained us to be leaders while providing the guidance we needed. They offered wise counsel, challenged us to make good choices, disciplined us when we messed up, and encouraged our growth.

Our parents have great wisdom, and they understand that true leaders produce other leaders. Remember that it takes leadership to stand for what's right when making the tough choices. So train your teens to shine as leaders among their peers!

The Why Behind the What

As the parent, you are not obligated to give your teens reasons for every rule you set or decision that you make. You do not owe them an explanation for every boundary you create. They should trust your decisions and obey, simply because you're Mom/Dad.

However, you've probably already noticed that human nature makes this tricky… Teenagers and adults alike are more inclined to make good decisions when they know *why* they're making the decision.

Let's discuss some simple examples:

Our mom always told us to drink a lot of water. We remember being elementary school age, and she forced us to drink a whole cup of this tasteless, filling substance! We complained that we were full and didn't want to finish it. And she told us that it was good for us and that we had no choice but to finish it. So we drank every drop. We obeyed.

When we read *The Seven Pillars of Health* by Dr. Don Colbert, we discovered that the human body loses about 2 quarts of water daily through perspiration, urination, and exhalation.

Because the body is 70% water, when your vital organs don't have enough of it, they steal it from other "less important" places, and then the problems in your body begin. Numerous health challenges can be avoided and cured through sufficient water intake, such as the following:

- Joint pains and arthritis
- High blood pressure
- Digestion problems
- Asthma
- Headaches
- Back pain
- Dry skin
- Allergies
- Heartburn
- Constipation
- Memory loss

After understanding the "why" behind the "what," we have much more motivation to drink 2-3 quarts of water daily! After all, if you're losing 2 quarts naturally, you also exercise, and you're not drinking enough, you're completely dehydrated. Now we know why our mom said to drink a lot of water, and we definitely don't need her to force us to drink a cup.

Because of her efforts, we learned to like water and drink it more than any other beverage. Consequently, we drink more water than most others we know. However, our motivation to increase our water intake and encourage others to do the same dramatically increased when we learned *why* water was so important.

Likewise, our mom told us to eat the colors of the rainbow. This means being intentional about incorporating all the different colors of fruits and vegetables, maintaining variety in your nutrition. Again, it wasn't until Dr. Colbert's book that we gained motivation to actually do so.

We discovered that each different color contains a unique phytonutrient, and various phytonutrients build your body's defense against different cancers, diseases, and disorders.

For example, watermelon, tomatoes, and red grapefruit

defend the body against heart disease and prostate cancer. Therefore, if you want your body to be resistant to all different types of infirmities, you need all the colors of the rainbow from your fruits and vegetables. This explanation turned on the light bulb for us!

The same principle is true for all the other wise decisions that you want your teens to make. Knowing *why* motivates *what* they decide. Why not get into the car with a stranger for a date, snort cocaine, get drunk, have premarital sex, skip school, hang out with troublemakers, procrastinate on assignments, stay out extremely late at night, disrespect authorities, and overeat?

Example:

"Did you know that overeating actually shortens your lifespan? Those who eat more meals in smaller portions are proven to live longer than those who eat fewer meals in large portions. Hmm…interesting."

Doesn't that paint the picture a little clearer, communicating the importance of eating in moderation?

Or even the whole curfew thing…

Man, it is such a shame that so many people are dying in car accidents because they were getting hit by drunk drivers. Those people were innocent, but they were just in the wrong place at the wrong time. There is a lot of crazy stuff that happens at night… Most drunk drivers are driving at night, a lot more crime occurs after dark, and the freaks come out at night! Really, people are more in the mood for sexual behavior at night. Even when people are trying to "set the mood" in a room, they turn the lights down. I fully trust you, but for safety purposes, it's wise to be back home by midnight so you're off the roads. And also avoiding late-night dates can help you resist sexual temptation.

Explanations like this help your teens understand why. This understanding provides incentive for them to make better choices, and consequently enhances their own decision-making abilities.

There are some values of yours that your teens will not adopt unless they understand the importance of the value.

When your teens do ask you why you made a certain rule, please avoid responding with the notorious, "Because I said so" (See "Discipline that Works."). In the moment, "Because I said so" feels like a quick, easy fix; but, in the long run, it's counter-productive. Try not to use that phrase just because you don't feel like thinking of an explanation.

If, as a parent, you feel like you don't quite know the explanation behind what you're teaching your kids, then look it up! We challenge you to put in a little extra effort to enhance the development of your teens. Help them learn your logic by explaining as much as possible.

As I (Kristie) mention in the "Discipline That Works" chapter, this one instance changed my mindset masterfully. When I was a teenager and upset about my mother's decision, she invited me to sit with her on the sofa.

She gave me a voice in this moment, or at least some illusion of a "say so" in the matter. She asked me to step into the shoes of a parent. "If you were in my position as your mother who loves you very much, what would you have done in this situation?"

"I don't know…" I replied.

"No, really, I want to know what you think," she said.

As I sat there and thought, it was almost frustrating how right she was. I eventually said, "Well, I guess I would've done the same thing you did."

My mother's wise decision to ask my feedback caused me to acknowledge a different perspective and aided my understanding.

I could no longer be mad at her for her decision because I completely understood why she made it.

Deciding Destiny

Beyond day-to-day decision-making, parents must learn how to let their teens make decisions concerning their own destiny. By the time teens reach the age for life-altering choices, you should be able to trust the values you've instilled and the decision-making skills you've developed in them. We've all heard of parents forcing their kids into paths that seem more fitting for the parent than for the teen. That's more like robot production than raising decision-makers.

As parents, you must realize that you are not *owners* of your teens, but you are *stewards* of their lives. Therefore, you cannot *create* your children's destinies. You can either nurture their God-given calling or divert them to a life of unfulfillment, trying to shape them into something they weren't designed to be.

For example, a particular parent-daughter relationship was strained because the parents tried to decide their daughter's major in college and her career. Their daughter felt like her passions and desires were unimportant to her parents.

They even sometimes spoke on her behalf to others, telling others her plans, which were really their plans. "She's going to be a doctor, following in her mom's footsteps!" they proudly stated. Their daughter felt suffocated.

She eventually decided to do what she felt in her heart to do, and she became much happier. She succeeded, too! As a result of her parents' decisions, she wasted time and became resentful.

Our parents, on the other hand, told all of us that we were going to college, and they explained why it is important in today's world. But they never pressured us, or any of our siblings, to attend a certain college or pursue a specific career.

Let's make the disclaimer that teens *do need* their parents' guidance. Our parents helped us to recognize our strengths that we were unaware of. They praised us for our talents, and they encouraged us to hone those skills, such as event planning. They even recommended a job they thought we'd be great at. But they never forced us. They only guided and encouraged us.

Sometimes, they asked us questions like, "What's in your heart?" But they never persuaded us to do anything to so-called "follow in their footsteps" or even anything especially lucrative, just for the sake of financial security. They also didn't rush us to decide what we wanted to do in life.

They encouraged us to pursue our God-given calling and corresponding passion(s), and they also taught us good financial sense. They certainly did not want us to blindly chase *any* dream. As a result, they taught us about financial consequences of career choices. They prepared us well to make the right decisions for the lifestyle that each of us desired.

They gave us wisdom and liberated us to make decisions, which demonstrated their confidence in us.

Our parents have very different personalities, so they've had to work together to remain consistent with this strategy.

Because he's Dad, our father has always been more of a natural when it comes to developing leaders, a.k.a. "decision-makers." He likes to ask us questions and guide us to the best answer instead of simply telling us the right choice. It seems easy for him to give us truth and sit back as we practice (a.k.a. "make our own decisions").

Mom, on the other hand, is quick to tell us what we should do. Her passion bubbles over, and she finds it hard to contain herself. Haha! But that's okay. Sometimes you should be frank with your teens. Both approaches are needed at the right times. So, whether you have a spouse or find a mentor for your teen, allow others to balance your weaknesses in order to provide the best development for your teen.

When you raise your teens with proper values, and you develop their decision-making abilities, trust them to make their own decisions. Even if you don't agree with their choices, you should share your advice and then let them come to their own conclusion. There is a consequence for every choice, so they will learn one way or another.

After all, parents are guardians, but not God. If not careful, parents will try to play God in their teens' lives, deciding their interests, passions, and careers for them. This can cripple teens, foster resentment, and possibly send them down unfulfilling paths. Share your wisdom, pray for them, and trust God to guide their destinies.

No More Training Wheels

At some point, the time must come when young birds are pushed out of the nest and given the freedom to exercise their own wings.

Once parents have instilled values in their teens and trained them how to succeed, they must allow their kids to make their own choices.

As we've stated, this helps teens discover what their true values are while they're still under parental supervision, and it also helps relieve some relationship strain. They get the opportunity to exercise their decision-making abilities in a safe place. If teens make the right choice and all goes well, they build confidence for themselves and for their parents. If they make a foolish decision and fail, they learn a memorable lesson.

We all know that parents must make some decisions for their children because teens don't always know what's best for them. But at a certain point in their development, begin to (1) share what you think is best, and then (2) give them the freedom to choose.

So, when you have trained your teens properly through a consistent example and intentional exercises, you can metaphorically take the training wheels off your kids' bikes and let them ride. No, it is not guaranteed that your kids won't fall, but as you allow them to exercise their decision-making abilities, they will grow stronger and stronger.

CHAPTER 10
THE "C" WORD

"You should be more like your sister. Stop just talking to all those boys and make some good grades for a change. Your sister is focused and will probably even be salutatorian. She is going places."

"See, Derek obeys his parents, makes straight A's, and aspires to become a doctor. Why can't you be more like Derek?"

"David is very respectful to authority. He's a nice young man, always saying 'Yes sir' and 'Yes ma'am'. I love David! You should learn something from him."

Many parents make these kinds of statements, thinking little about the effect.

No one feels good about being the negative counterpart to someone else's success story, the black backdrop to another person's shine. And that's what comparison feels like! For some reason, parents seem to think that comparison will serve as the motivation their teen needs.

In reality, it makes teens think that their parents don't view them as highly as they do the person they're being compared to. They, then, feel like rebelling, giving up on striving for some faraway standard. Like, "That is Megan, but this is me!" This bitterness can cause them to intentionally resist modifying their behavior to resemble the person you are referring to. Think about how you feel when your spouse compares you to one of his/her ex's, telling you to do "xyz" more like he/she did. Not the way to go…

Comparison feels belittling and discouraging. It also strains the parent-teen relationship and often affects the teen's attitude towards the person that he/she is being compared to. Telling your teen to be like someone else can cause unhealthy competition, jealousy, or bitterness towards the assumed "competitor." In fact, this comparison can actually thwart your teen's effort altogether.

Additionally, negative comparisons can sow seeds of discord in your home. Imagine the effect of making these comparisons among siblings: How does that affect their relationship? Also, parents sometimes compare their teens to the parent's younger self: "When I was your age, I used to…" We will further discuss this concept later in this chapter.

Basically, comparison doesn't accomplish what you'd hope. But rather, it discourages. This chapter will shed light on often-neglected topics surrounding comparison, while offering solutions to help you motivate your teen.

One Too Many

Growing up, our parents often compared us to other kids, but in a positive way. They would say things like, "You all are so much wiser and more mature than the other kids your age," and "None of your friends do 'xyz'—you're exceptional." Our parents did a great job of not comparing us to others in a negative way; however, there was one memorable mistake…

We knew another pastor's family that we occasionally spent time with, and the five kids of that home were very wholesome, like the five of us. They were homeschooled, morally exceptional, intelligent, sexually pure, and very spiritual at young ages.

One big difference between our lifestyles and theirs was that they loved reading, while we loved television. They would actually get in trouble for reading too much, which was hard for us to understand! One of them told us the following funny story:

"One time, it was past my bedtime, and my parents had already told me to stop reading and go to sleep. I wanted to continue reading so badly that I took my book with me to the bathroom, sat on the toilet, and pretended to be pooping for quite a while!"

We thought, "Wow! What a daredevil, sneaking to read! What a NERD..." We, nor our siblings, identified with their passion for reading because, at that time, we thought of recreational reading as a geeky activity. TV was our kind of fun! To us, watching TV for hours after we did our homework was normal and maximally entertaining.

To this day, we remember riding in our large, white van, heading home from our visit with this family... We started talking about these kids' love for reading, and we became intensely annoyed. As we voiced how boring we thought that sounded, Dad responded with something like, "You all should read more like them. That's exceptional, the way those kids love to read! They don't even have a TV in their house. Watching all that TV isn't good anyway..."

This made us roll our eyes (in our head, of course, so we wouldn't get in trouble). And if you were wondering, no, we did not start reading more. We didn't even try. We only built our reading habit many years later when we felt inspired to do so.

At that time, we instead started thinking, "Man those kids are such goody two-shoes!" And we felt offended to be compared to them at all.

That was the first and last negative comparison that we can remember from Dad.

If we so vividly remember one comparison that was made when we were around eleven years old, how much more offended do teens get by comparisons their parents make on a regular basis?

Parent-to-Teen Comparisons

"You have some big shoes to fill."

"When I was your age, I made straight A's all the way through. I was at the top of my class. You better come up!"

"You have a lot to live up to."

"You're pretty good, but you don't do it like your mom."

"You're all right, but your dad *really* knows how to…"

Beware of comparisons that pressure your teens to conform to your image. In the process, you can provoke them to do the exact opposite, just to relieve themselves of that pressure. This struggle often leads to rebellion. Your teen is actually seeking to create his/her own identity, even if it's not a good one. Basically, when pushed, teens will go the extra mile to be different from you, just to prove their independence.

What can be more dangerous is comparing your teen to yourself or to his/her mom or dad when you find negative similarities.

"Wow, Son, I see you've got that weakness for women like me."

"You sound just like that lying mom of yours right now."

"Your dad never could keep his word, and here you go breaking your promises too."

"Keep eating like that, and you'll be fat just like your mom!"

"You've got that smug, arrogant look on your face, just like your father."

Comparisons like these can make your teens feel like they're doomed to repeat the mistakes of their parents. What better way to make them *not* believe the best in themselves?! If you can convince them that it's in their genetic makeup to be selfish, rude, or any other negative trait, you can provoke their habits to be just that!

Although it is likely that your teens will display negative qualities resembling yours, vocalize who you want them to be instead of just what you see.

Sometimes, you'll have to speak the exact opposite of what you see and convince them of that. Be determined that, even if no one else sees the good in them, you do. Encourage them to be who they can be, who you want them to be, rather than emphasizing the negativity that might be most evident. Shape their futures positively with your words. (See "Powerful Language.")

Saving Sibling Relationships

Parents often think that they are simply highlighting a great example, when, in reality, they are degrading a relationship. Comparing your older son to your younger son, for example, might seem like a clear, tangible illustration; but, instead, it breeds discouragement.

Parents often have good intentions, but their motives might be perceived very differently by their teens. Take a look at what one student had to say because of her parents' comparison of her to her sister: "...I always saw myself as the black sheep... I wasn't good enough or smart enough to get to the level of my sister who is younger than me."

We've heard numerous students admit that their parents' seemingly constant comparisons make them think that their parents love their sibling more than them. Most times, this is not true. But in any instance, parents should always avoid making comparisons that could lead their teen to believe that.

Because of parents' comparisons of their kids, sibling relationships are sometimes damaged. One teen said, "I don't even know why God made you the oldest. I'm more mature than you." The only reason that this teen made this harsh statement is that she was mirroring her parents' open and constant comparison of their maturity.

Sometimes, people underestimate the comprehension level of teens. The same way that kids naturally pick up on your mannerisms, accents, facial expressions, and behavior, they observe other details about you and the way you handle things... including the ones you'd hope they miss.

When you give one kid more chores than the other, whether intentionally or accidentally, they notice. We definitely paid attention to the number of chores our brother had in comparison to our load.

One of the easiest ways for parents to strain their teens' relationships with each other is to show favoritism.

Despite the gender difference, we thought it was only fair to make chores equal. When we noticed inequality, we fussed about it to our mom, and sometimes, our brother was present during those exchanges.

For obvious reasons, our brother was never happy about our convincing Mom to give him a longer chore list. Although we have a good relationship with our brother now, small things in our childhood caused tension.

Another inequality that we hated as kids was our mother promising to spank all of us for a particular violation but failing to follow through when it was her only son's turn! (Keep in mind that he was not just the only boy, but also the youngest of the bunch.)

For example, she said that no one could wait until morning on the way to school (elementary) to complete homework. Our brother disobeyed her commands whenever it was convenient; however, he remained more "spanking-free" than all four of his sisters (who did their homework on time)!

Needless to say, we, as the most vocal among our sisters, nagged our mother constantly about this injustice! Once again, our parents' mistakes induced strain on our relationship with our brother.

Of course we looked at our brother funny when we felt he deserved many punishments he never received. And, he enjoyed liberties that we were not afforded! And naturally, he resented us for always reminding Mom to punish him. We tried to assist her by finding the most painful belt, and as he got older, by recommending specific privileges that he loved most to be taken from him. Haha!

One of the easiest ways for parents to strain their teens' relationships with each other is to show favoritism. It's obvious that we had wonderful parents, but no one is perfect... Our parents are well aware that we've felt like they gave our brother special privileges. Disclaimer: They probably don't agree with us 100% on the severity of their favoritism, but we're just sharing our perspective 😊.

We can so clearly remember an instance of favoritism when we were in elementary school... The "Rugrats" movie was coming on at 8:00 p.m. on a school night, which was our bedtime. When we asked Mom if we could stay up and watch the movie, she quickly replied "no."

Out of our eagerness to see this movie, we ran to our brother and persuaded him to ask Mom for us. We told him something like, "We know she'll say yes when you ask her because she always says yes to you. Can you please ask her if the three of us can stay up and watch it?"

He agreed, and we listened outside the door for her response. He asked only one time, and she sweetly answered him something like, "Of course, Sweetie Pie." (She conveniently doesn't recall this, by the way!)

To no surprise, we were hurt, offended, and outraged that she would blatantly give us a different answer from our brother. Although we were happy that we were able to watch our movie, the perceived favoritism was unhealthy for our sibling relationship.

As we grew older, more offensive instances arose. When we were about fourteen years old, our brother (3 years younger than us) felt ready for his first cell phone, although we were fairly indifferent about having one. In his youngster wisdom, he realized that the best way to get Dad to buy him a cell phone was to persuade him to buy our phones first.

He convinced our father by persistent comments like, "It's not safe for young girls like them to be out with no cell phone! What about if they get in danger and are not near a pay phone or don't have any coins for a pay phone? It's only safe for them to have cell phones." The underlying motive was this— "While you're already at Verizon, you might as well get me one too!" Thus, we got our first cell phones so that he could get his. He succeeded!

He got his first laptop before we did, as well as whatever game systems he begged for. When it came to receiving our first cars at driving age, our dad made extremely economical decisions for us and our older sisters.

He got their cars from auctions, and we got ours free from our uncle when he was ready for a new one (Yes, the two of us shared a car!). We all passively stood by and gratefully received whatever our father gave us. After all, it was a car, and it was free!

Our brother, on the other hand, took our dad to a car dealership and persuaded him into a "good deal" on a used luxury car, a black two-door Infinity sports car. Even though we were perfectly content with our car that we received at sixteen years old, we couldn't help but compare our vehicles to his when our brother turned sixteen and received a luxury car.

To be honest, we didn't desire to have a car like that, but we thought it was unfair for him to have one. We figured that we were all young, inexperienced drivers, and we all deserved to have cheap cars for a while!

Whenever we'd complain about inequality, our mother would say, "You have not because you ask not. Your brother receives certain things because he begs for them and is very persistent. If you want the same things, ask for them."

Honestly, we didn't feel comfortable asking for a lot because we figured that we were already given plenty.

Again, although we have a wonderful relationship with our brother now, after we've all matured, it was challenging for years because of what we perceived as favoritism. Resentment doesn't always pass with time, though; so parents, definitely do your part to avoid this situation.

As the parent, be mindful of giving your teens equal chores, regardless of one's cleaning ability over another's; bestowing equal gifts, of comparable value; maintaining standards among all your kids, even if some are more persuasive than others; balancing compliments in an equally affirming way; and following through with whatever punishment you promise to all, so discipline is fair.

Also remember that teens' communication styles are different: just because your teen doesn't voice his/her preference or opinion does not mean that he/she will be okay with siblings receiving more. Sometimes, your teen doesn't feel comfortable asking for certain things because he/she feels like it's too much to ask, while another child is bold enough to ask for anything.

Be sensitive to your teens' differences, and be careful not to display favoritism. Remember to get in their heads and ask questions. When you know what they're thinking, you can clarify misconceptions. That way, they're less likely to misinterpret your motives or resent one another.

Balancing Praise

I (Kirstie) can clearly remember feeling jealous and discouraged when my parents raved over Kristie's handwriting during our penmanship class in middle school. I felt bad because I secretly craved their compliments for my work. Instead of feeling motivated to work harder in the class, I felt sad and discouraged. (Keep in mind that I was a very conscientious and competitive child, and I acknowledge that kids are different.)

Although this instance wasn't an example of a direct comparison, and our parents were totally pure in their motives, this demonstrates that parents should be careful to balance compliments among their children whenever more than one is present. Our parents were usually great at this, particularly because they had five children, two of which were twins—Anyone with twins knows that comparison and competition are a big deal!

One way to avoid celebrating one child more than another is to give certain compliments to your teen in private if you think it might make his/her siblings feel insecure in comparison. Judge this case by case, as it is also beneficial to publicly affirm your teens.

Additionally, be intentional to recognize the differences between your kids in more ways than one, because there is something to celebrate in everyone!

Okay, so Jim excels academically. What is Ryan good at? There must be something. Instead of focusing on the strength of one child and the corresponding weakness of another in the same area, find the strengths in both, whether obvious or obscure.

Ryan might be so creative, such an out-of-the-box thinker, that he is unorganized, sloppy, and might even seem lazy. If you compare him to Jim, it could seem that he is the inferior son. But if you look a little closer, you might notice that Ryan is great at creative solutions, unconventional ideas, writing music and short stories, painting, and a host of other things that don't require an "A" in mathematics.

When you are tempted to celebrate the strengths of only one or some of your teens, take the time to think of the strengths and talents of even your "special" child so that you make all of your kids feel celebrated.

The teen who always questions you and maybe even challenges some of your decisions could be the lawyer of the future if someone took time to teach him how to channel this gift. Encourage that teen in his ability to analyze and help him see the value in his natural bend.

Some care-free spirits who seem nonchalant about everything can be a tremendous asset to an uptight friend or spouse someday.

Our parents did an excellent job of recognizing and celebrating the various gifts in their kids. As a teenager, our oldest sister didn't have the best discernment in choosing friends. She kind of welcomed anyone without weighing the pros and cons of that person's character.

Instead of calling her naive, our parents chose to emphasize how Dalina saw the best in people and encouraged them through anything. She made people feel great about themselves, even if no one else did. Although our parents did advise her concerning who she should date and befriend, they also took the time to regularly celebrate her positivity.

Our brother has always been strong-willed and even stubborn sometimes, but our parents recognized and encouraged his gift of leadership, which he now uses to help others. That stubbornness now means that he is uncompromising in his values.

And our sister, Neiel, was always emotionally and spiritually sensitive and shy. As a teenager, this caused her to be moody and antisocial sometimes. But our parents encouraged her speaking and writing gifts that they noticed. Now, she is a phenomenal writer (which you need solitude for), prophetess (which you need sensitivity for), and preacher!

Always celebrate every gift so that all of your teens feel valuable to you, despite their individual differences.

The Solution

"Look, Sweetie, you can be whoever you want to be! You can change as soon as you desire to. You have endless potential, and I believe in you. You're intelligent, and you simply need to put in more effort in school. You can do it, though! You'll be surprised how much you can do when you put your all into it. You will be unstoppable!"—Motivation from an Encouraging Parent

Instead of comparing, simply encourage! As the parent, you might think you need to use the example of someone else, but in reality, old-fashioned motivation is all they need!

> *Even though you don't know what you want to do in life yet, always know that whatever you choose, you can work hard, pray hard, and be your best! Keep seeking God and paying attention to your passions to discover what you should aspire to. Keep doing your best in all you know to do on the level where you are, and you have nothing to worry about!—Motivation from an Encouraging Parent*

Your encouragement will push your teens further than any

comparison ever could. When you imagine being the "wind beneath their wings," notice that air provides support and necessary pressure for the wings to fly, but it's enjoyable at the same time. Birds love to fly on columns of air!

In contrast, imagine putting knives under their wings, seeking to motivate flight by the pain of falling. Yes, the birds might try to rise above the knives and fly, but the journey will probably be short-lived and miserable.

Think of your teens as the birds, your encouragement as the wind, and your comparisons as the knives. Inspire your teens to be their best, to soar high and enjoy the journey.

CHAPTER 11

CREATING YOUR FAMILY CULTURE

W hat if you could sit and daydream, envisioning what you want your family to represent... How they would behave, what values they would embody, and what your family's legacy would be... What if you could then give your kids tunnel vision for those very things?

Think about it: For everything that people deem maximally important, they lay the groundwork for success through careful planning and written goals. They don't just go with the flow and hope for the best.

Every successful business or organization establishes clear values, a slogan, a mission statement, and detailed plans for best results. They create a business plan to establish their brand, the culture of their team, and a plan of action.

For example, Chick-fil-A's slogan is "Eat More Chicken," and its mission statement is "To glorify God by being a faithful steward of all that is entrusted to us. To have a positive influence on all who come in contact with Chick-fil-A."

As a result of this intentionality, many comment on Chick-fil-A's excellent customer service, friendly employees, good food, and observation of the Sabbath. They make more money six days of the week than many other chicken chains make in seven! They are clearly successful. Some people might wonder how a fast food place is so exceptionally positive, how they stand out above the rest... Well, they planned for it!

An excerpt from an August 2012 article reads as follows:

> Chick-fil-A is a family-owned and family-led company dedicated to serving the communities in which we operate. From the day Truett Cathy started the company, he began applying biblically-based principles to managing his business. For example, we believe that we are stronger because of such principles as closing on Sundays, going the extra mile in service, treating others as we want to be treated, and devoting a percentage of profits back to our communities.

Take notes from Truett Cathy and the brand of his business as you consider how to clearly define who you are as a family.

Another example is Apple, Inc. Apple's slogan is "Think Different," and its mission statement (2015) is the following: "Apple designs Macs, the best personal computer in the world, along with OS X, iLife, iWork and professional software. Apple leads the digital music revolution with its iPods and iTunes online store. Apple has reinvented the mobile phone with its revolutionary iPhone and App Store, and is defining the future of mobile media and computing devices with iPad."

As you can see, Apple's mission statement is very specific. When reading it, you can clearly recognize the company's identity and goals. Their success has been planned. Should families not also be specific when deciding their culture and direction?

Steve Jobs' original mission statement for Apple, Inc. was "To make a contribution to the world by making tools for the mind that advance humankind."

This mission has also been accomplished. The whole world recognizes Apple as a tech world-changer, reinventing the cell phone, personal computer, and more: Undoubtedly, this company has advanced humankind with exceptional tools that will leave its mark in history.

Businesses like Chick-fil-A and Apple clearly have not been successful by accident, nor did they enter new realms of greatness blindly. They had a plan; they wrote their vision; they clearly defined their company's brand; and they worked hard to realize the vision.

● ● ●

With planning and passion, treat your family like the most important business you could ever have.

● ● ●

With planning and passion, treat your family like the most important business you could ever have.

The best businesses have a distinct culture that is composed of atmosphere, customer service, and quality product. How is the atmosphere of your home; how do you treat each other (customer service); and, what kind of product/behavior comes from your home? Create your family's culture with specificity, aiming for excellence in its design. Decide who you will be and how your family will primarily be characterized.

Creating Your Culture

The first step to branding your family for success is to brainstorm and write a list of what you want your kids to value. Write everything you can think of that's important. This list should be very long and should take you about 20 minutes to draft.

Sample Brainstorm:

- Having and maintaining a close relationship with God
- Obtaining a good education
- Making good decisions
- Honoring and trusting God

- Being a person of integrity
- Handling money wisely
- Honoring your mother and father
- Keeping your commitments
- Having respect for God, self, authority figures, and others
- Being free and confident to be yourself
- Keeping quality friends who bring out the best in you
- Studying scripture
- Living a balanced life of work and clean fun
- Being a leader
- Giving to help the less fortunate
- Abstaining from sex until marriage
- Being positive
- Applying wisdom
- Abstaining from pornography
- Being responsible
- Pursuing your dreams
- Giving tithes and offerings to God (via the church)
- Being sensitive to others' feelings, even if you don't understand them
- Maintaining your health through physical fitness, a nutritious diet, and adequate sleep
- Working hard and smart
- Being grateful and saying "Thank you" regularly
- Not living to impress people (the only opinions that matter: your opinion of God, His opinion of you, and your opinion of yourself)
- Being honest and transparent with trustworthy people in your life
- Treating others the way you want to be treated
- Being humble

From there, write your family mission statement. This will add focus and brevity to your family values.

Sample Family Mission Statement:

To impact the world with love, innovation, and passion by empowering a unified household of pure-hearted leaders.

Next, write your family creed. This family creed is a focused list of values that serves as a charge to your family. You can write this creed in the form of "Household 10 Commandments," bullet points, or a paragraph. Try not to make it so long that your family will be too lazy to periodically read it. And be creative!

Sample Family Creed:

"In the Johnson household, we always…"

- Forgive quickly
- Communicate respectfully and openly
- Hug often
- Serve Jesus Christ faithfully
- Give generously to each other and to those in need
- Invest in our personal passions/aspirations
- Encourage and compliment regularly
- Express gratitude often
- Eat healthily and exercise consistently
- Lead powerfully
- Maintain sexual purity
- Tithe faithfully to God
- Live with integrity
- Radiate joy daily
- Love unconditionally

Remember to include your teens in the process of creating your mission and creed. That way, they feel a sense of ownership and are more likely to value your family plan.

Whatever you write, take time to adequately revise, frame, and post in visible places in your home.

Lastly, when you're building your family's foundation, consider what you experienced in your home growing up that you did or did not like. Imagine what would have enriched your life more, what you wish you had, and determine to give those experiences to your children. And don't feel the need to reinvent the wheel: Repeat the things your parents did well!

On Your Mark, Get Set...

Now that we've established the importance of creating the overall vision for your family, we want to suggest specific concepts to consider, things to intentionally teach them. Of course there are numerous lessons to share with your teens. But we suggest you cover these topics in addition to the ones we've already discussed throughout *Bridging the Gap*:

Relationships

Parent: "When did you start spending your whole check on everything BUT your responsibilities?! And since when are you being all closed off? You won't tell me anything anymore these days, and I'm finding stuff out from your Instagram! One day I think we're good, and the next day I find out you're cheating on your math quizzes, smoking, and God knows what else!"

"You were doing well. Who stopped you from obeying the truth?" —Galatians 5:7 (NLV)

One of the most fundamental values you should instill in your family should be choosing the right relationships. One friend, girlfriend, or boyfriend can alter your teen's moral compass, financial decisions, and overall attitude. Relationships can even affect your teen's eating and exercise habits.

That's why it's important to specify clear guidelines regarding friendships and romantic relationships. What qualities do you want your teen to embody? Would you be okay if your kid turned out just like his/her best friend? Make sure your teen's relationships reflect those qualities and reinforce the right values.

Concerning *falling* in love, do you really want your teen to *fall* in love or to *decide* who to love? Every day, we see people falling in love with those who mistreat them or serve as poison in their lives. It just *happened*. People seem to have no kind of control. That should not be the case.

People can choose to open their hearts intentionally at the right time and to the right person. They do not have to fall in love with just anyone who makes them feel good at the moment.

The Bible says, "Guard your heart above all else, for it determines the course of your life." —Proverbs 4:23 (NLT)

Our mom always taught us to guard our hearts. She also reminded us to be careful of how much time we spent with certain people. She'd say, "If you spend enough time with just about anyone, you can develop feelings for him."

Teens should know that dating is not a sport, but its purpose is to find a suitable spouse. Therefore, teach your kids not to initiate romantic relationships with people who do not possess the integrity they need in a husband or wife.

Any close relationship will change your life. The question is, how? So help your teen choose wisely.

Keep in mind that having quality friendships and romantic relationships at the right time are amazing additions to life. Living a life of isolation is not only boring, but emotionally, spiritually, and mentally draining. We were designed to be in relationships with other people. That's why people who live "hermit-like" existences often seem strange and underdeveloped.

Encourage relationships with the right people in the right context, and your teen's life can be enriched rather than de-railed.

Emotional Health

In addition to healthy relationships for your teens, it is vital to consider their emotional and mental health. For this, teens need the freedom to be themselves and to express themselves in their own home.

At school, work, and internships, people often feel like they have to wear a certain mask. They wear these masks for a number of different outcomes—to be accepted, to gain respect, to seem professional, to appear strong, and much more.

But at home, masks shouldn't exist because suppressing negative emotions makes the heart toxic. Cultivate an environment of transparency so that everyone in your household knows that they have your permission to express themselves freely.

The best way to create this culture in your family is to use strategic language with your teens and to respond appropriately to honesty.

"Sweetie, tell me what's on your mind. Good or bad, I want to hear it, and you can always tell me anything."

"How was everyone's day? Honestly. We won't think you're complaining. This is a safe space to vent: we're family."

Make sure your teens understand that, as long as they remain respectful, you are willing to listen to whatever they need to share.

When your teens express themselves, remain calm and understanding, even if what's being said is in some way disappointing. In the moment, focus on being a good listener and a source of comfort. One of the reasons we loved talking to our parents about whatever was going on in our lives is that they were great listeners and very supportive. They also did not overreact.

If you need to correct something, wait a moment so that your teen feels understood first. Later, you can say something like, "Hey, Buddy, I really appreciate your sharing with your mom and me. We want to be there for you through the good and the bad because that's what families do. Next time, though, please watch your tone. You might not have meant it this way, but your tone came off disrespectful. We have to always remain respectful in this house, even when we are having a hard time."

It could be that you don't agree with something they say when they're sharing with you. Still, let them have that moment and simply be supportive. Wait until another time when they aren't as emotional. Then approach them with your concerns.

Example:

Ryan, when you were telling us about how your friend punched you the other day because you went out with his girlfriend, I wanted to let you know that, although I completely understand you being angry and fighting back, in the future, you should consider what things can look like. If you were him, you would've been upset if you thought your friend was betraying you. Even though you weren't pursuing her romantically, taking her to dinner alone was a bad look. So if you want to thank her next time for helping you with a test, invite a group, and especially be sure to invite her boyfriend.

You are free to be honest, also, but consider timing and approach so that you **seek first to understand and then to be understood**. This way, your teens won't be as defensive, and they will be much more prone to receiving your correction and counsel. They will also be less likely to regret sharing with you in the first place.

Make your home a haven, a place of rest and rejuvenation for the soul. Do your part to keep the minds and hearts of your family members clear by giving them a safe outlet, a place where their confessions won't be used against them or be distributed as the latest gossip. And what better place than home?

Moral & Spiritual Compass

Parent: "As long as you keep those A's and remain on the honor roll, I'll make sure you get your weekly allowance and keep your cell phone. I'm proud of you Kayla, keep up the good work!"

Kayla: *["Dang, I don't know if I can finish strong in this Calculus class… I might need to look on Andrew's paper just one more time."]*

Academics are undoubtedly important to many successful careers. But is that the most important element of your teen's life? If you believe that true success is more than that, be sure to emphasize more than just schoolwork.

● ● ●

Seek first to understand and then to be understood.

● ● ●

When leading your family, consider the following concepts:

- Accomplishments or integrity?
- GPA or honesty?
- Trophy or spirituality?

There doesn't have to be an "either, or," but rather "both, and"! The problem is that too many parents are not emphasizing the inward traits above the outward accomplishments. What happens in these scenarios is that students study for their tests but don't pray or read their Bibles.

They cheat on their tests because their parents' approval is more important than their personal integrity. Somehow, in their minds, the end justifies the means. Parents, take a closer look at the celebrities of Hollywood that are depressed, addicted to drugs, and divorcing multiple times: Understand that trophies don't always mean true success.

With your words and actions, you must show your teens what they should value most. For example, on a difficult test, they should study hard and do their best; but, if their best is a "B-," that's better than copying their neighbor's answers for an "A" they didn't earn.

Concerning a healthy sense of morality and spirituality, look beyond what's most visible when you encourage and correct your teens. If you only acknowledge the visible things, you'll exclusively encourage success in athletics, academics, organizations, etc. A physical trophy and a scholarship mean nothing if he/she is a lying, cheating, lazy, and immoral teenager. Integrity should always be priority.

Finances

"Why does David have a new pair of $200 sneakers when he can barely even pay his cell phone bill?"

"Why is Sarah always getting her nails, toes, and hair done professionally when she can't even afford to pay for car insurance?"

Financial problems limit opportunities, induce stress, and often even destroy marriages. Equipping your teens for financial stability will enhance their quality of life and enable them to help others.

One of the greatest lessons about finances that our father taught us is to "live beneath your means." Simply put, don't spend money just because you have it. Your expenses should always be far less than what you earn. And save plenty for emergencies.

Being frugal is not always fun because you're considering needs over wants. However, the "fun" thing about living a frugal lifestyle is that you don't carry the same amount of stress as someone who has no money to spare when his car breaks down or when he gets laid off from his job.

Over-spending to impress people is not worth the stress and struggle. Instead of focusing on being flashy, be smart. Would you rather just *look* rich or *be* rich? Let your spending habits reflect your answer to that question.

Our father also taught us not to lend anything we cannot afford to lose. Why? Because sometimes you won't get it back! And you can't afford to give something that you are dependent upon. If you can't pay your bills until you get the money back, you should not lend it. Also, unpaid debt destroys many relationships. Because you lent money to a friend, expected it back, needed it, and struggled as a result, you became resentful.

However, this does not mean being stingy. Our parents taught us to give the first 10% of all the money we get to God. Therefore, we gave some of our birthday and Christmas money to the church as far back as we can remember, and we still tithe today. God blesses us as a result, and we never miss that money.

We also give to others. An integral part of financial responsibility is generosity. We are blessed to bless, and every gift is intended to be given. Be sensitive to whom you can help whenever you are able: you never know if one day that person could be you.

What perspective of money do you plan to transfer to your teens? Is money simply a tool to get material needs and wants? Is money a necessity to make you feel powerful? Is money connected to self-worth and personal value? What does it mean to worship money? What does it mean to simply respect money? What is the value of giving your money to help others?

Establish what's more important than money, where money should be among your priorities, and how you should use it. If you aren't intentional about how you frame your teens' perspective of money, they will likely resort to a default view. This default view could be yours, or it could be the general public's view, as materialistic and foolish as that might be.

As you ponder how to convey the value of money to your teens, first evaluate your own mentality. Are you a good steward of your finances so that God can trust you with more? Do you value saving, investing, and multiplying your money? What is the purpose of money?

Answer these questions honestly for yourself and decide how you want your teens to view money.

If you find that you need to make changes in your own financial value system, then do it. That way, your teens can have the *best* view rather than a default view.

Let wisdom guide your family's financial decisions, and avoid making frivolous choices that build debt, stress, and can eventually destroy relationships.

Related Scriptures:
- Deuteronomy 8:18 (NLV)—But remember the Lord your God. For it is He who is giving you power to become rich...
- Proverbs 11:24-25 (NLT)—Give freely and become more wealthy; be stingy and lose everything. The generous will prosper; those who refresh others will themselves be refreshed.
- Luke 6:38 (NLT)—Give, and you will receive. Your gift will return to you in full—pressed

down, shaken together to make room for more, running over, and poured into your lap. The amount you give will determine the amount you get back.

- Proverbs 6:6-11 (NLT)—Take a lesson from the ants, you lazybones. Learn from their ways and become wise! Though they have no prince or governor or ruler to make them work, they labor hard all summer, gathering food for the winter. But you, lazybones, how long will you sleep? When will you wake up? A little extra sleep, a little more slumber, a little folding of the hands to rest—then poverty will pounce on you like a bandit; scarcity will attack you like an armed robber.

- Malachi 3:8-10 (NLT)—Should people [rob] God? Yet you have [robbed] me! But you ask, "What do you mean? When did we ever [rob] you?" You have [robbed] me of the tithes and offerings due to me. You are under a curse, for your whole nation has been [robbing] me. Bring all the tithes into the storehouse so there will be enough food in my Temple. If you do, says the Lord of Heaven's Armies, "I will open the windows of heaven for you. I will pour out a blessing so great you won't have enough room to take it in! Try it! Put me to the test!" (*Note: This translation uses the word *cheat*, but we replaced it with the word *rob* that many other translations use.)

The Body

Although your body isn't everything, you need it because you only get one of these while on Earth. No "do-overs" in that department! Poor health is not only uncomfortable, but it is also a distraction from your life's mission. It wastes time and reduces quality of life.

Remember that your teens have a great destiny to fulfill, and they can do much more if they're not frequenting a hospital bed in their forties. Habits are hard to break, and they'll catch up with you someday. So train them for long-term benefits during their formative years.

Many health challenges can be prevented, by having good daily habits. An ounce of prevention is definitely worth more than a pound of cure in this case.

For example, if you just minimize stress in your daily life, you can avoid many stress-induced diseases and disorders. Believe it or not, enjoying your life more now will give you a more enjoyable life later! Why be unhappy now and even more unhappy when paying the price for those negative emotions?

If you want to steer your family in the direction of great health, be sure to explain to them the "why" behind the "what," as discussed in section 2 of "Raising Great Decision-Makers." If you don't know, try looking it up and do your best. Dr. Don Colbert's book *The Seven Pillars of Health* provides a phenomenal foundation.

Most people know all the basics of good health but just don't practice them because they aren't motivated enough. For example, everything that's in the following list is very simple, and you've probably heard it a million times. But take a moment to evaluate which ones you actually follow regularly:

- Diet
    - Eating plenty of fruits and vegetables
    - Drinking lots of pure water daily
    - Avoiding genetically modified foods
    - Eating sweets and fats in extreme moderation
    - Avoiding fried foods and sodas
    - Taking multivitamins
- Exercising 3-5 times per week
    - Cardio
    - Strength training
    - Stretching

- Sleeping adequately
  - 7-9 hours per night
- Living a balanced life
  - Taking annual vacations
  - Reserving a sabbath every week
    - No work
    - No errands
    - No obligations
- Keeping stress levels low
  - Breathing deeply
  - Establishing stress relievers in your daily life

Not much new information, right? The key is to value health enough to do what you know to do. Accordingly, guide your teens in that direction so they can live long lives with great strength, energy, and overall health.

Identity that Lasts

You'll find that, once you've established the culture of your family, you will have a much stronger family identity. Your values, mission, creed, and heightened focus on what's important will make your family's legacy rock-solid. Remember, creating a plan for your "family business" is guaranteed more success than proceeding haphazardly.

Also, defining who you are as a family is one of the greatest gifts you can give to your family for generations to come. Imagine if you build something so powerful that your teens stand upon a firm foundation, standing taller than you ever did, and then give their kids an even greater platform!

An old saying says, "A short pencil is worth more than a long memory." The more you write down (and LIVE), the more easily transferable your values are. The blessing of a strategically written plan is that it's designed to last beyond the first hands you place it in, and your kids can more easily pass the baton.

● ● ●

Your family is the greatest legacy you'll leave.

● ● ●

Remember that **your family is the greatest legacy you'll leave.** Not only will your kids and grandkids carry the values you've instilled, but they, along with the generations they'll birth, will touch many other lives with what you've created. They will multiply pieces of YOU in the world, so be intentional about what that looks like. **Build your family as the greatest business you'll ever own, and trust that your investment will change the world, one family at a time.**

CHAPTER 12

HEALING FOR MOM AND DAD

P ain to purpose; mess to message; sorrow to story; test to testimony; worst to wisdom… and the list goes on. You, as a parent, might have an extensive past, many skeletons in your closet. You might feel wounded from a traumatic childhood, a drama-filled divorce, the death of a loved one, a life-changing disability, or a world of other disturbing challenges.

You might've just seen poor parenting examples in your home growing up, and you've ended up repeating some of the same behaviors that were harmful to you.

The harsh reality is that hurt people hurt people. You've probably heard this many times, but it's not until you see clear examples that you understand what this really means.

An individual can have pure intentions in his/her heart towards a loved one and still end up hurting that person because of the inevitable! **You cannot love someone else properly without first loving yourself, and you cannot give what you do not have.**

Therefore, if you are broken, you will more than likely raise broken teens. Although you love them, you could hurt them in ways you'd one day regret.

Understand this: When we discuss brokenness, we are not

● ● ●

You cannot love someone else properly without first loving yourself, and you cannot give what you do not have.

● ● ●

just referring to a person who experiences pain. Everyone experiences pain. Our definition of a "broken" person is someone with open wounds, metaphorically speaking.

Open wounds are vulnerable to germs (easily offended & overly sensitive), and when someone accidentally touches the open wound, the "broken" person lashes out because of the pain. This "lashing out" is how "hurt people hurt people."

Our definition of a "healed" person is someone with scars. Although the source of pain was once an open wound susceptible to infection, it is now a scar that represents a story. When people get close to someone with a scar and accidentally touch that scar, there is no pain, only a story of pain and restoration.

The hope is this: There is healing available for every broken person, despite age. No matter how long your wounds have been open, they can always be closed. You are not doomed to suffer with the same pain that you've been bearing your entire life.

Some think it's selfish for parents to focus on themselves. But they need time to pursue wholeness and evaluate the example they've seen in their home growing up. That way, they can decide what to repeat and what to discard. Otherwise, they cannot offer their best to their teens.

In this chapter, take time to reflect on yourself, your experiences, and your parents. Reflect, discuss, pray, and seek wholeness that will yield greater peace for you and a better parent and spouse for your family.

"Time" — An Incompetent Healer

Just because the saying says that "time heals all" doesn't mean we're guaranteed that toxic emotions will simply disappear over time. People often assume that adults need less help because time has passed since childhood traumas occurred. The myth is that old wounds aren't a big deal anymore.

In reality, it is quite common for people to shove significant moments of pain to the back of their minds, hoping to forget. According to psychology, it is sometimes a natural bodily response to forget very traumatic instances in childhood because the brain enters self-defense mode. It is easier for a child's brain to protect itself by blocking out certain memories than it is to deal with them. Kids don't have the emotional capacity to deal with certain levels of trauma.

While this phenomenon is more common in children, many adults intentionally strive to suppress their most emotionally taxing memories. They hope to gain some temporary peace and "move on" with daily tasks.

People only fool themselves into thinking that they've moved on. Just because they have stopped crying, and their body has continued habits of going to work, eating, sleeping, dating, and even laughing does not mean they've healed.

What seems to have faded into the background often maintains subconscious influence from "behind the scenes." And, yes, that influence yields harmful consequences.

Imagine a 32-year-old man who had a rough childhood of physical and verbal abuse, molestation, and rejection. He is promiscuous, seeking temporary pleasure in numerous women, hoping to forget everything that caused him pain. Drunkenness, clubs, sex, and marijuana fill his time when he's not at work. He has never shared with anyone about his damaging childhood experiences.

He thinks he's okay because he manages to keep smiling and cracks a lot of jokes, acting as the life of the party. He also thinks he has moved on from his past because he never cries. It hurt so much and so often that he silently taught himself how to *not* feel. He has become hardened and emotionally insensitive.

Unfortunately, after he gets married at age 35, he still doesn't feel anything. His wife complains often about emotional neglect and detachment because he doesn't let her into his heart. The same wall that he built many years ago to block the pain now serves to block his wife as well.

His defense mechanism activates immediately when he realizes that she could hurt him, and he refuses to be transparent. He remains emotionally withdrawn and chooses to distract himself from the lack of emotional intimacy with pornography.

Because his wife is now the only one emotionally present in their marriage, the passion fades. Her husband feels safe within his walls because that's his comfort zone.

He finds himself becoming nonchalant and not even desiring restoration of the marriage. This is because he subconsciously chose not to care when he erected his emotional walls. It was a habit.

Within 10 years, the married couple feels like nothing more than distant roommates, and the only reason they haven't yet divorced is their two children. These two kids are also hurt because their dad has never said the words, "I love you," and he doesn't even hug them. He only buys them things. Mom finally decides that the whole house would be happier if they divorced. Consequently, their kids feel rejected by Dad who's no longer around.

This story could have ended the same way even if this man had *not* gone the emotionless route. What if he had allowed himself to continually feel the pain, still without healing? He would have been haunted by his past. Being haunted by dreadful thoughts would have impacted his marriage and parenting differently, but still negatively. Instead of shutting down and not talking, he could have overreacted to every complaint from his wife with yelling, profanity, and possibly even physical abuse. And instead of ignoring his kids, he could have been aggressive towards them.

When someone is haunted by negative thoughts, they can become overly sensitive to current circumstances. While his wife would have been confused and offended by how dramatically he responded to simple comments, he would have felt like her comments served as the last thing to push him over the edge. Over and over, he could allow tiny annoyances from her to magnify his inward conflict, building on his unresolved issues.

Imagine a kid standing on top of your large luggage at home: **Every problem looks taller when it's standing on top of baggage you already have lying on the foundation of your life.**

The problem is that unresolved issues remain unresolved if ignored. Time alone is an incompetent healer! Distracting yourself from the problem can potentially push the problem into your subconscious instead, but it still affects you. When you don't recognize how it affects you, you can wrongly blame other circumstances and people. **You must become aware of why you feel the way you do in order to change your feelings and behavior.**

If self-hatred and insecurity are allowed to fester in a mother, she can then become that mom who tells her daughter, "You ain't cute, and you ain't smart either!" We've seen this happen when the daughter was the spitting image of her mom, and the mother hated herself. Consequently, she could not properly express love to her daughter.

Or what about demonstrated favoritism toward one teen over his/her sibling? One of them reminds you of yourself at that age, headed to your dead end, and the other has a more disciplined and studious personality... Remember that **you hate in others what you can't stand in yourself.**

Also, we've probably all seen a parent criticize his/her child saying, "You're just like your no-good dad! You're nothin' and you never will be nothin'!" Where does this come from? Does it actually stem from the identity of the teen or from the mother's unforgiveness toward her "ex"?

You must become aware of why you feel the way you do in order to change your feelings and behavior.

If there's a lot of dirt in your house, the dirt doesn't go away just because you hide it by sweeping it under the rug in your living room. Eventually, the dirt will build up and start creating bumps under the rug. People will trip over these bumps and some will fall. Soon, there will be so much dirt under the rug that there won't be enough surface area to contain it, and it will spill beyond the rug's edges.

The issues of our lives, when left hidden and untreated, are just like the dirt in this metaphor. Other people will experience conflict (trip) with us, without seeing the real problem. The issues under the surface are the ones that need to be fixed. Trying to flatten out the bumps in the rug will do no good when the same dirt is still underneath. Flattening out one bump will only form bumps in other areas. Eventually, what is hidden will be revealed, and it won't be pretty.

As much as you might want your issues to disappear, ignoring them will only cause them to be displaced. Let's look again at the following story from "Productive Mind Games" within "Powerful Language." This is a powerful example of displaced issues:

> "You're ugly, and you're stupid, and you're selfish, and you're unkind!" [Silence] "And you still haven't changed your attitude! And you're not even sorry." [More silence] "You are just like your daddy," the mother yelled, this time with the sound of tears welling up in her voice. "Just go, just go!!! Go get in the d*mn car and let's get the h*ll out of here!"

The first time we told this story, the focus was on the negative words that the mom spewed at her daughter, but this time we want to focus on the reason for her outburst.

It is very clear that she was filled with pain and plagued with voids. Her own life's frustration provoked her to verbally abuse her daughter. By her words, "You are just like your daddy," it is clear that she didn't have a good relationship with her daughter's

father and was still highly emotional about it. Her voice shook
while she spoke those words,
followed by uncontrollable tears
when her daughter left the dressing
room.

In this story, her daughter's
feelings could have been spared if
the mother had sought healing in
the following areas, instead of try-

> *Emotionally healthy people who love themselves are better equipped to love others.*

ing to shove them in the background and move on with daily life
(without *really* moving on): 1) unforgiveness towards her daughter's father and 2) a lack of self-love. If she loved herself like she
should, she wouldn't have attacked her daughter's self-
stomaimage the way she did.

Parents, if you don't heal, you will continue to have experiences that elicit pain from the past. Therefore, it is vital to your
teens' health that you pursue healing.

Notice we say *pursue* healing. Healing does not happen on its
own, but you must take purposeful and consistent action until you
become whole. We discuss tips for healing later in this chapter.

The Selfishness of Pain

Let's face it: pain is selfish! Pain screams out for relief for itself, not others. That doesn't mean that people who live life broken don't care about others. But it does mean that **emotionally
healthy people who love themselves are better equipped to
love others.**

Look inside yourself and be honest. Be real. Are you yelling
at your teen so much because he/she is really that annoying, or is
some of your anger due to your own challenges? Do you slap
your kids so hard because their mistakes are adding onto the
frustration you're already carrying? Do you find yourself occasionally snapping on your teens because they just so happened
to be the last straw that topped off your already bad day?

Parents naturally want to give to their kids, not take from

them. They want to help, not harm. They want to be selfless so they can properly sacrifice for their children.

So why is it that parents don't always display this kind of love and actually *do* harm their teens? The answer often lies in the selfishness of pain.

Too often, we have seen parents who don't love themselves damage their relationship with their teens because they don't know *how* to love their kids. Again, you cannot love someone else properly without first loving yourself.

We watched a movie (*Two Guns*) that had an interesting line in it related to this topic. In the movie, a man and woman are in bed together as unofficial sex buddies. They don't have a romantic relationship because the woman loves the man, but the feeling isn't mutual. Longing for his love, she sincerely asks him, "Did you ever love me?" He frankly states, "I *meant* to love you."

Although that reply can be confusing, we understood exactly what he meant. He was an emotionally guarded man who didn't fully love who he was, since he was deceitful and hardened. He didn't want her getting too close to him for fear of hurting her. And he didn't feel capable of loving her the way she needed him to, although he deeply cared for her.

The only reason that people become hardened in their hearts is that they have been hurt so many times that they've erected walls around their hearts in self-defense.

Although they don't intend to hurt anyone, people get hurt in the process of their protecting themselves. In this movie, the male character hurts the woman because he's so hurt, although he genuinely *wants* to love her. He is keen to the reality that he desires to love but cannot.

Unfortunately, most people are not able to recognize and articulate their disposition of *intending* to love but literally being incapable of properly doing so. Most people in this predicament try with all of their might to bypass the vital step of first loving themselves.

A common example is absent fathers. Often, when a father

refuses the opportunity to have a relationship with his child and remains distant, the father doesn't feel good about himself.

He might feel like, "She'll/he'll be better off without me. It's not like I have anything to offer to this kid anyway. I'd be doing him/her a favor to just disappear." Although these aren't thoughts that men usually vocalize, they are real sentiments.

Kids often blame themselves for their father's absence when the father's self-image is the real issue.

Sometimes, the absent father feels like the best thing he can do for his children is to protect them from himself. His own pain can ring so loudly in his life that, as much as he wants to love his kids, he can only hear the cries of his own heart.

How can you give something you don't have? How can you express love properly when you don't know how to love yourself?

One daughter painfully admitted that her mother didn't make her feel loved. She acknowledged that her grandmother did the same thing to her daughter (this teen's mom). Because this teen and her mother were both single moms, they experienced similar life struggles that toughened them. Instead of this commonality bringing them together, the mom grew bitter and pushed her daughter away.

Out of her mother's pain and pride, she broke her daughter down to tears during an argument, using these words: "I don't want a relationship with you!"

She never apologized for that or retracted her statement. After several attempts from her daughter to strengthen their relationship over the years, she made it clear that she did not want to be close with her daughter. Only hardness caused by severe pain could provoke a mother to intentionally reject her daughter.

Because her mother didn't love herself or like her physical appearance, she refused to take pictures with her daughter or grandson over the years. Into her twenties, her daughter still didn't have any pictures with her mother! This situation is not about a despicable child, but rather a broken parent.

Additionally, sometimes, hurting parents literally leave their teens to carry their emotional burdens. They treat their kids as their confidants, and the teen might even feel that he/she is responsible for taking care of the parent.

"My mom is suicidal and pushes her depression on me. She sees me like a father, a brother, a boyfriend and a husband and then… like her son. I supported and saved her from her suicidal thoughts, but when I tried to kill myself, she wasn't there." — Anonymous

This mother likely didn't mean to communicate to her son that she didn't care about him, but she was just so distracted by her own pain…

The selfishness of pain can be hurtfully appalling when it affects those you want to love the most.

Generational Parenting

Have you ever noticed your parents' methods reappearing in your parenting style? It is often true that you become what you behold, meaning that you imitate the behavior you repeatedly see, whether consciously or subconsciously.

A prime example of harmful patterns trickling down from one generation to the next was revealed through interviews we conducted with a mother and daughter, separately. The mother shared that her father's favorite word for her sister was "stupid." As a result, her sister thought she was dumb for a long time.

Because the mother was overweight as a child, instead of her father celebrating with her when she made the cheerleading team, he asked, "They let you on the team, with your size?!" She replied, "Yeah, they let me on as an alternate."

Talking to her daughter, we discovered that her mother calls her stupid regularly. When asked if she feels like the repetition of the label "stupid" affects her behavior, she quickly responded "yes."

Her daughter felt like she could never meet her mother's standards, like nothing would ever be good enough. She also felt like her mother overreacted so intensely that she wasn't able to voice her opinion. "She gets mad over anything," she said. She simply wanted to be heard, but her mother's lack of self-control prevented her from having a voice in her home.

The mother admitted to fussing and yelling a lot because her father was, in her words, a "yeller." Like him, she sometimes felt like her teens weren't listening until she started fussing, yelling, and cursing.

When parents are emotionally wounded, they are much quicker to lash out at their teens during challenging times. Therefore, it is important that this mother first forgive her father and seek healing through God and counseling. Then, she can learn to properly love herself. Consequently, she will automatically be better equipped to love her daughter.

It is also important to identify what was negative about your upbringing and to be intentional about making positive changes. Before she had kids, the mother in the above example should've evaluated the damage her father's words caused and, therefore, determined to take a different approach to her own family. Some successful parents have admitted that, after evaluating their upbringing, they decided what things they would never repeat and what they would do instead.

For example, one particular mother said that she wished her mom had talked to her about sex and relationships in detail in order to prevent some heartbreak. Her older sister was great at giving her bad advice, and her mother was wise, but just too reserved to discuss the "hot topics."

Before she had kids, this daughter decided that she would be open with her teens in ways that she wished her mother was with her. By the time she had teens of her own, she was so transparent about relevant teenage issues that she became characterized by her openness and wisdom. She succeeded in helping her teens avoid many of the mistakes she made.

Additionally, identify what your parents did well and decide if you will continue those habits. Consider what your parents did, or someone else's parents, that made you feel loved, appreciated, and celebrated. Also consider what boundaries were beneficial to your development. **Repeat effective habits, not mistakes.**

Many negative habits that pass on and on from parents to their children are generational limitations upon that family's line. Some call that a *generational curse*. For example, Susan's grandmother conceived a child out of wedlock and was never married. Susan's mother did the same thing, and now Susan, a 16-year-old girl, just discovered that she is pregnant, and she is unsure who the father is.

Another example is that Joe hit his wife for the first time last week under the influence of alcohol, and he is terrified of himself because he hated his father for being an abusive alcoholic.

Remember that any limitation can be overcome, even if it is generational. Decide that it will end with you and take corresponding action.

Generational behavioral patterns unevaluated and uncorrected often breed dysfunction; but, recycled wisdom and intentional improvements build stronger families.

The Effects of Self-Hatred

When we were teenagers, we were at a recreational outing with the youth choir at our church, when we were faced with a very disturbing problem…

A teenage girl appeared extremely sad. When one of us went to help her, she revealed that she was sulking because of her low self-esteem. She felt like she was truly hideous!

When we inquired why she felt so strongly about this self-hatred, she responded explaining that her own mother told her that she is fat, ugly, and stupid.

Although she struggled with anger and unforgiveness towards her mom, she believed the words that her mother repeatedly spoke.

What we found to be shocking was that, although this teen girl was only slightly chubby, her mother was much more overweight than she was. Also, in the face, the mother and daughter looked almost exactly alike!

This demonstrated to us a prime example of how parents'

self-hatred can cause them to manifest disgust for the similarities they find in their teens. This makes kids feel unloved, and they think that their parents hate them, when really they are displaying disdain for themselves...

We discovered months later that this hurting girl had performed sexual favors for a couple of guys during the outing. If we had focused only on her actions, we definitely would have missed the glaring problem. We could reprimand her misconduct and judge her, or we could lovingly correct her and address the underlying issue.

How many other teenagers are displaying destructive behavior because of issues no one has taken the time to notice? Because the mother didn't love herself, her daughter didn't love herself either. As a result, numerous challenges arose. And unfortunately, this is just one example of many.

Also in our teenage years, at youth choir rehearsal, we witnessed another painful example of this concept. We were talking to a girl in the hallway that was new to the choir, probably her first or second day. She must've been hurting desperately because she proceeded to tell total strangers her life's story...

She expressed that her mother hates her and favors her sister. We assured her that her mother loves her, but just fails to express it properly. She continued to explain that her mother's praise for her sister and disdain for her made it obvious who she loved and who she didn't.

Some people might think that the favorites game is not a big deal. But consider this: When a child feels unloved, no matter what the cause, he/she will seek this love in other places. You would hope they'd seek God for it, but sadly, that's unlikely.

This teen girl soon became pregnant. She was the talk of the youth ministry. A couple of years later, she became pregnant with her second child. Then, she began an even darker and more perverse sexual path.

This broken child was not a slut, but merely a hurting girl seeking healing through love. She sought love through attention from boys during sex. She sought it through her infant's need for his mother. And she sought a mother's love through sexual relationships with other women.

We were heartbroken to discover that it was only self-hatred that caused this girl's mother to push her away as she did. This mother's heart was broken over her daughter's condition. But she subconsciously sabotaged her daughter because looking at her reminded Mom of all that she hated about herself.

We discovered that her mother was also once a promiscuous teen mom. And she had also sought a mother's love through sex with other women. What's more is that she, too, had a bad reputation as a teenager because of her notorious sexual activity.

Clearly, her bias towards her other daughter stemmed from the pain of watching this daughter become her. A generational limitation was definitely in effect.

Many parents who struggle with self-hatred are actually trying desperately to keep their teens from becoming who the parent is. These very efforts suffocate their teens, push them away, and breed resentment.

The Road to Healing

Parents are people too, and all people need wholeness for healthy relationships. Understand that self-condemnation is unproductive, and negative focus intensifies the problem. Therefore, don't beat yourself up.

We acknowledge the voids and wounds of parents, along with the corresponding consequences, only to expose the need for change. Awareness is the beginning of change, and now is the time to evaluate, improve, and move forward empowered.

Don't look backward in shame, but look forward in hope. Let your remorse about yesterday fuel your efforts tomorrow. One step at a time, one day at a time, seek restoration.

Often, people overlook the most effective source of healing because they are so focused on the things they see around them. The first step to healing is to seek the ultimate Healer.

God is the one who can heal your soul better than anything

else because He created it. He knows the details of your inner design unlike anyone else ever can, and He holds power and wisdom beyond imagination. Nothing is impossible for God (Luke 1:37 KJV).

Seek God through daily conversation, called prayer. Tell Him what is on your mind and heart and listen to what is on His. He has answers that the best doctors or psychologists couldn't give you!

Read the Bible. It's actually the best book in the world. It holds truth that is more entertaining than fiction and power that can transform your heart, mind, and circumstances. Select the scriptures that encourage you the most, and memorize them. Consider the source of your brokenness, and find scriptures that speak to that issue. Meditate on them. Let them become part of you. Below are some examples:

Fatherlessness/Motherlessness:

Even if my father and mother abandon me, the Lord will hold me close. —Psalm 27:10 (NLT)

Discontentment:

… I have learned, in whatsoever state I am, therewith to be content. —Philippians 4:11 (KJV)

Depression:

The Lord is close to the brokenhearted; he rescues those whose spirits are crushed. —Psalm 34:18 (NLT)

Why are you sad, O my soul? Why have you become troubled within me? Hope in God, for I will yet praise Him, my help and my God. —Psalm 42:11 (NLV)

Worry:

6 Don't worry about anything; instead, pray about everything. Tell God what you need, and thank Him for all he has done. 7 Then you will experience God's peace, which exceeds anything we can understand. His peace will guard your hearts

and minds as you live in Christ Jesus. —Philippians 4:6-7 (NKJV)

³ You will keep in perfect peace all who trust in You, all whose thoughts are fixed on You!

⁴ Trust in the Lord always, for the Lord God is the eternal Rock. —Isaiah 26:3-4 (NLT)

... ²⁵ Do not worry about your life... —Matthew 6:25-31 (NIV)

Doubt:

⁵ Trust in the Lord with all your heart; do not depend on your own understanding. ⁶ Seek His will in all you do, and He will show you which path to take. —Proverbs 3:5-6 (NLT)

Discouragement:

So let's not get tired of doing what is good. At just the right time we will reap a harvest of blessing if we don't give up. —Galatians 6:9 (NLT)

Unforgiveness of yourself:

If we confess our sins, He is faithful and just to forgive us our sins, and to cleanse us from all unrighteousness. —1 John 1:9 (KJV)

¹¹ For His unfailing love toward those who fear Him is as great as the height of the heavens above the earth. ¹² He has removed our sins as far from us as the east is from the west. ¹³ The Lord is like a father to His children, tender and compassionate to those who fear Him. ¹⁴ For He knows how weak we are; He remembers we are only dust. —Psalm 103:11-14 (NLT)

Unforgiveness of others:

For if you forgive other people when they sin against you, your heavenly Father will also forgive you. —Matthew 6:14 (NIV)

Anger:

And don't sin by letting anger control you. Don't let the sun go down while you are still angry. —Ephesians 4:26 (NLT)

Low self-esteem:

I praise you, for I am fearfully and wonderfully made. Wonderful are Your works; my soul knows it very well. —Psalm 139:14 (ESV)

Rejection:

[14] For all who are led by the Spirit of God are sons of God. [15] For you did not receive the spirit of slavery to fall back into fear, but you have received the Spirit of adoption as sons, by whom we cry, "Abba! Father!" [16] The Spirit Himself bears witness with our spirit that we are children of God... —Romans 8:14-16 (ESV)

... He made us accepted in the Beloved. —Ephesians 1:6b (NKJV)

The Bible is full of life, hope, and strength! But without relationship with God, the Bible, to you, is more like historical poetry than power for living. And without God, there is no hope in this life. So we encourage you to take a moment to reflect on your life and on eternity.

(1.) If you have not yet received Jesus Christ as your Savior, (2.) if you've fallen away from God, or (3.) if you're just not sure where you stand with Him, we encourage you to pray the following prayer:

I believe in my heart, and I confess with my mouth that Jesus Christ is Lord. He died on the cross for my sins and rose from the dead three days later. I now accept Christ as my personal Lord and Savior. I forgive everyone whom I have bitterness towards, and I ask that You forgive me for my sins. I renounce every generational curse/limitation in my family and declare that it ends with me today, in Jesus' name. I release soul-ties with anyone that is not in line with Your will for my life. Thank You, Lord, for Your grace and for saving me. Help me to grow daily in my relationship with You through consistent prayer, Bible study, and relationship with other believers. Change my desires to match Yours, and teach me Your ways. Heal every part of me that needs healing and fill me with Your Holy Spirit. Make me new in You (2 Corinthians 5:17). In Jesus' name, amen.

Now that we've covered the most important part, let's discuss a local group of believers—the church. If you're not already connected, get involved in a church that you feel is the right atmosphere for your growth. Start serving and helping others, which builds character in you and changes your perspective of life.

As you get involved, you can connect with positive people and gain accountability, good counsel, and emotional support. You always need a good accountability partner to discuss regular struggles and how you are responding to those challenges.

In addition to healthy friends, find a person you admire to mentor you. Everyone should have at least one trusted person in his/her life to offer wise counsel. No matter how long you've been living, there's someone else who has more insight on some things than you do, especially since omniscience is only characteristic of God.

Even our mentors have mentors, and that is a demonstration of their great wisdom. Your mentor can be anyone from your pastor to a mature friend. Whoever it is, give him/her permission to be honest with you and correct you when necessary. When you have the right people teaching you, you can go much further than you ever could alone.

Keep in mind that your mentors are also human, so you will inevitably be disappointed if you expect perfection. Set realistic expectations, and pray that God brings the right people into your life.

The room for improvement is the biggest room in the world, and those committed to continual learning have the greatest opportunity to reach their fullest potential. **We must all be hungry enough to seek wisdom and humble enough to receive it.**

Also, read relevant books that can teach you through the experiences and wisdom of others.

Lastly, never be embarrassed to get counseling if you need additional help, especially if you've experienced emotional trauma.

The road to healing is quite a journey, but you must be committed to pursue it. Through wholeness, you can give your teens all the love that your heart intends. Remember, if you want to raise healthy teens and have healthy relationships with them, seek healing for your brokenness. And then, once those open wounds have healed, don't hide the scars. Share your stories of pain and victory when the time is right. You'll be amazed by the wounds you can heal and by the scars you can prevent for your teens by showing them yours.

●　●　●

We must all be hungry enough to
seek wisdom and humble enough to receive it.

●　●　●

CHAPTER 13
AFTER YOU'VE TRIED

"Train up a child in the way he should go, and when he is *old* he will not depart from it" (Proverbs 22:6 NKJV). Hearing this verse, you might be thinking, "Why would the Bible say that my teens won't leave the good foundation I've laid for them? It looks to me like they already have! I've worked hard to teach them well, and I feel like they've forgotten all the good sense I gave them! What did I do wrong?!"

For some reason, we usually understand this scripture to mean, "Train up a child in the way he should go, and when he is old he will *never* depart from it."

Have you ever noticed that sometimes good parents have a seemingly "bad" child, and then years later that same kid appears to transform? Think of Bishop T.D. Jakes' daughter, Sarah, for example: She had a baby at fourteen years old and later wrote a book called *Lost and Found* to celebrate her redemption. She now teaches others how to grow from their mistakes and turn failure into fuel for a better future.

It's important to understand that, when you've done your best with your teens, raising them in the ways of the Lord, God has not promised you that they would never rebel. But, He has promised you that they won't be lost forever. Just because your teens don't live righteously in their youth doesn't mean that they will die in those rebellious ways. Mistaking God's promises can result in severe discouragement, so be clear and be encouraged!

Some people have to learn the hard way, but that does not mean they'll never learn.

Also, don't blame yourself or God for every rebellious act or phase in your teen's life. Sometimes those moments call for parental re-evaluation, but other times it's just a natural part of life.

At times, you have to stand strong and remember that, when your family serves God, your teens are not just yours, but God's. You are only their steward.

Consider praying a prayer like this: "God, this is Your child, so please give me wisdom to handle him the right way, and give me peace as I wait for his return to the foundation I have laid."

Relinquishing Control

You should be relieved to know that your teen's rebellion is not always your fault! Take a look at this:

> *I used to be the wild child because it was just in me. It was nothing my parents did wrong. They did a great job actually! I clearly knew the difference between right and wrong, and my parents repeatedly told me, "We trust you." I knew they told me that to hold me to a higher standard. It was just that I didn't like to be controlled or told what to do. I wanted to do my own thing. I wanted to try things for myself, even though I knew that drinking, smoking, and premarital sex would horrify my parents if they knew. —Anonymous College Student*

Some teens have a tendency to pursue their own experience over the wisdom of someone else. You might call this "hard-headed" or "stubborn." The point is that **some people have to learn the hard way, but that does not mean they'll never learn.**

In light of this truth, sometimes you have to be patient and wait for your teen to come to his/her senses.

As a parent, this process of waiting can feel like torture. We've watched many parents suffer, itching for the day that their teen will turn around. In no way do we intend to belittle how real that struggle is. It's a natural part of passionate parenting. We're simply suggesting that you do the only constructive thing you *can* do: Have faith in God and in your teen. **Pray, wait, and never give up!**

One teenager's parents tried to guide their daughter the best way they knew how. Apparently, they were pretty competent because their other three kids were exceptionally pure and responsible. But for some reason, their daughter just felt like she had to so-called "see for herself" and make her own choices, against her parents' counsel.

The truth is that her personality never changed. Even as an adult, she sometimes still ignores wise counsel until something bad happens. But she has gotten much better. She has fully dedicated herself to God, decided to live wholesomely, and devoted her life to helping others. Her personality causes her to bump her head more than she has to and experience more heartache; but nevertheless, she is learning, growing, and on the right path. Her stubborn nature actually proves useful, as she stands firmly for righteous causes, despite opposition.

Trust God and relax. Although it's easier said than done, don't lose sleep over every issue with your teen. Remember that God is sovereign and in ultimate control of everything. **As soon as you stop trying to control everything in your life and the lives of your family members, you'll regain peace that you have lost.**

Pray, wait, and never give up!

Peace, sleep, and rest for your soul are the gifts you gain when you let go of stress, worry, and control-freak tendencies. Realize that you cannot control everything, and worry is the opposite of trust.

You can begin "letting go" through prayer. Pray for your teens. The Bible says, "Give all your worries and cares to God, for He cares about you" (1 Peter 5:7 NLT). As a parent, your teen's cares become yours as well. You can also lay those on Jesus and enjoy a better quality of life.

And Philippians 4:6-7 (NLT) says this: ⁶Don't worry about anything; instead, pray about everything. Tell God what you need, and thank him for all he has done.⁷Then you will experience God's peace, which exceeds anything we can understand. His peace will guard your hearts and minds as you live in Christ Jesus.

Through prayer and gratefulness to God, you can have peace despite your circumstances.

Why hold tension in your body over things that aren't in your power to change beyond prayer? Again, it's definitely easier said than done, but it's not impossible.

When you've done all you can do, give it to God in prayer and let it stay in your prayer room: don't keep carrying it.

Pray detailed prayers for your teens. The same kind of detail that you would use complaining to your spouse about your children's behavior is the same kind of detail you should use with God. Tommy Newberry said this: "Take your nags to God before you take them to anyone else."

As you spend time in prayer about the details of your teens' lives, you'll find that you have less need to complain, and you'll notice positive results in your teens. Prayer is a powerful tool that too many people leave unused. You'll be surprised at the prayers that God will answer for you, even if you're not the most spiritual person on the block. Give it a try!

Comparing Parents

As our father always says, **"Don't compete, don't complain, and don't compare!"** As parents, it's easy to compare your teens to other people's kids who are well-behaved, academically successful, and spiritual.

Our oldest son, Brad, just graduated from Harvard University and is now working full-time for NASA. He just got married to a doctor named Kelly and is expecting his first child. Our youngest daughter, Amanda, is a straight-A student at Whitefield Academy and is a virgin who loves spending time with her family. Oh, and she's captain of the debate team at school.

"Oh wow, that's great... We're hoping our 24-year-old Alex will go back to school sometime soon... He's really smart, just needs some motivation. And uh, our 16-year-old Ashley is pregnant with our first grandchild, so we're just hoping for a healthy baby..."

When you compare your teens or parenting skills to those of others, you are taking a big risk—you will either end up feeling superior and proud or embarrassed and discouraged. Simply focus on your own family and don't pay too much attention to the households of others.

The only exception to this is mentorship. If you find another family that serves as an inspiration to you, then by all means, study that family!

But don't compete: only love and learn.

Love & Let Go

Your teens might not always be star students, but they'll always be *yours*. So be proud of them and love them for who they are. Your love and support will go further than you know.

● ● ●

As our father always says, "Don't compete, don't complain, and don't compare!"

● ● ●

Some of you might feel out of control of who your teens have become. No matter what you do or say, it seems you can't change them. Focus on loving them, just for who they are.

As much as God wants the best for our lives and wants us to follow His lead to become our best, one thing never changes—His love. **Let your love remain constant even if your teens never change. If you master nothing else about parenting, learn to love your kids faithfully, fiercely, and openly, so they always know.**

● ● ●

If you master nothing else about parenting, learn to love your kids faithfully, fiercely, and openly, so they always know.

● ● ●

ABOUT THE AUTHORS

K irstie (Bronner) Foley and Kristie (Bronner) Brawley are youth and young adult pastors, youth event coordinators, authors of *Double Vals: The Keys to Success in College and Life Beyond*, and the founders of Elite 31 mentoring program at Word of Faith Family Worship Cathedral in Austell, Georgia. They are passionate about inspirational speaking, mentoring young ladies, developing leaders, and leading worship as vocalists.

Kirstie and Kristie were born and raised in Atlanta, Georgia. Kristie resides in their hometown with her husband, Brandon Brawley, founder of Infinite Empire, LLC and The Brawley Agency. Kirstie currently lives in Germany with her husband, Captain Kyle Foley, who serves as a U.S. Air Force C-130J pilot. She works for Word of Faith remotely and commutes for special events. In August 2019, Kirstie gave birth to her first child, Elaina Stephanie Foley.

Ask questions, share testimonials, and invite Kirstie and Kristie to your events through their website www.kirstieandkristie.com or email them at info@kirstieandkristie.com.

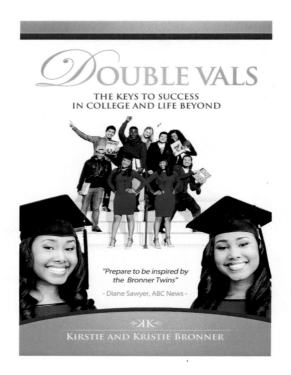

Kirstie (Bronner) Foley and Kristie (Bronner) Brawley graduated from Spelman College in 2013 as the double valedictorians with matching 4.0 GPA's. In *Double Vals*, Kirstie and Kristie share the secrets to their success in college, which they still use in life today. Join them as they colorfully illuminate their college journey infused with powerful keys that will enrich your daily habits!

You'll learn the keys to…

- Study tips that work miracles
- Time management that makes you a master of minutes
- Scheduling that conquers busyness

- Relationships that boost your GPA
- Perspective that redirects your focus
- Excellence that causes you to stand out
- Risks that you *should* take
- Balanced living that yields holistic health
- Classroom miracles that drop your jaw
- School lessons that transfer to life lessons

Purchase *Double Vals: The Keys to Success in College and Life Beyond* on www.kirstieandkristie.com.

$15.99 Paperback
ISBN 978-0-9891356-8-9

 CARNEGIE BOOKS